THE CUNNING
OF FREEDOM

THE CUNNING
OF FREEDOM

SAVING THE SELF
IN AN AGE OF FALSE IDOLS

RYSZARD LEGUTKO

Encounter BOOKS

New York • London

First American edition published in 2021 by Encounter Books,
an activity of Encounter for Culture and Education, Inc.,
a nonprofit, tax exempt corporation.
Encounter Books website address: www.encounterbooks.com

Manufactured in the United States and printed on
acid-free paper. The paper used in this publication meets
the minimum requirements of ANSI/NISO Z39.48–1992
(R 1997) (*Permanence of Paper*).

FIRST AMERICAN EDITION

LIBRARY OF CONGRESS CATALOGING-IN-PUBLICATION DATA

Names: Legutko, Ryszard, 1949– author.
Title: The cunning of freedom : saving the self in an age of false idols /
Ryszard Legutko.
Description: First American edition. | New York : Encounter Books, 2021.
Identifiers: LCCN 2020008128 (print) | LCCN 2020008129 (ebook)
ISBN 9781641771375 (cloth) | ISBN 9781641771382 (epub)
Subjects: LCSH: Liberty—Philosophy. | Self (Philosophy)
Classification: LCC B824.4 .L45 2021 (print) | LCC B824.4 (ebook)
DDC 320.01/1—dc23
LC record available at https://lccn.loc.gov/2020008128
LC ebook record available at https://lccn.loc.gov/2020008129

Interior design and typesetting: Bruce Leckie

CONTENTS

INTRODUCTION

The question of freedom has engaged me ever since I first seriously immersed myself in the study of philosophy. On several occasions in the past I had thought I was ready to tackle the subject methodically only to discover to my dismay that, once I started pulling all the threads of thought together, I was not. The question of freedom first entered my life as a theoretical problem, as is natural for any philosophy student who reads the standard texts from Plato, to Hegel, to John Stuart Mill. For me, however, freedom was primarily a practical problem, the acuteness of which I experienced almost daily. Most of my life was spent in the People's Republic of Poland, a country and a system in which freedom was scarce and the desire for it immense. Painful restrictions on speech, action, even thought, marked just about everything that took place in school, at university, and in my social and academic life; and almost everything I desired required those restrictions to be lifted. Inevitably, my intellectual inquiries turned enthusiastically towards books and essays on freedom in the hope of finding a language in which I could articulate a theoretical account of my experience, and which could somehow save me from my wretched situation. I learned much from those writings yet, with hindsight, I see that the external circumstances of those times, which became increasingly harder to bear, made me expect far more from those books than simple intellectual exercise–that is, far more than they could offer.

Living in a Communist country made me increasingly aware of the flaws, inaccuracies, and plainly false conclusions that could be found in some of the concept of freedom's major interpretations which, initially, had greatly impressed me. I remember how surprised I was to discover that Isaiah Berlin's famous essay on two concepts of liberty, which once inspired many Polish intellectuals, myself included, was nothing more than a collection of platitudes and falsehoods that prevented rather than encouraged any serious reflection on freedom. In reality, Berlin's essay claimed it would be politically dangerous to make stronger assertions regarding metaphysics or the philosophy of human nature because these could lead to, or at least justify, the restriction of freedom. Whoever made such strong assertions was, in Berlin's words, "in a position to ignore the actual wishes of men or societies, to bully, oppress, torture them in the name, and on behalf, of their real selves."[1] He explicitly stated that several of history's most important and profound philosophical thinkers either willfully or unintentionally created ideas that could be used as intellectual weapons against human liberty. "Can it be," he asked, "that Socrates and the creators of the central Western tradition in ethics and politics who followed him have been mistaken, for more than two millennia, that virtue is not knowledge, nor freedom identical with either? That despite the fact that it rules the lives of more men than ever before in its long history, not one of the basic assumptions of this famous view is demonstrable, or, perhaps, even true?"[2]

I considered Berlin's affirmative answer to this question an absurdity, all the more pernicious as it soon turned into a cliché that authors of all abilities repeated until it acquired the status of unassailable wisdom. How many times have we heard that when we talk of truth we pave the way for the alleged truth-holders to keep dissenters in concentration camps? Or, when we talk of virtue, we prepare the theoretical ground for imposing severe discipline on those sinners and moral weaklings who engage in vice, pleasure, and frivolity instead of moral self-improvement? I told myself that if we pursued this line of argument we would have to conclude that a gigantic intellectual purge would need to be conducted for freedom to exist. Such a purge would tarnish Western philosophies' core theories as politically suspect for being either covertly or openly authoritarian and totalitarian. Indeed, some authors less gallant than Berlin did not hesitate to say so in a most blunt and repugnant way. As for Berlin himself, he eventually noticed his essay's disconcerting consequences and attempted to refute some of his assertions. But the original text has remained intact and has continued to exert its harmful influence.

I did not care for this philosophy of freedom while living under Communism; later, once that system had collapsed, I liked it even less. In an independent, liberal democratic Poland, the debate about freedom lost its seriousness, as it did throughout the entire Western world. I could see that in the ongoing crusade for freedom and liberties (which never lost its ideological dynamic) the scope of our view on the subject was rapidly shrinking, not expanding. Nor could I fail to notice that the set of problems encompassed within the word "freedom," which Communism reduced considerably, continued to decline further once that ideology was gone. This led me to the rather frustrating conclusion there was no place for myself in the debates being conducted during that period. The concept of freedom got into the hands and minds of dogmatists who turned it first into a rigid, ultimately fruitless formula, and then into an ideological tool to promote a liberal model of society that I found increasingly dubious. So, I decided to rethink the concept of freedom once more, taking inspiration from the classical philosophical tradition in the belief that, in the light of this tradition, the cunning of freedom would reveal itself more fully. In defiance of Berlin, I believe the concept of freedom should open us up to an abundance of weighty philosophical questions about the world and our place within it, rather than discourage us out of fear that we put our freedom at risk by answering those questions.

PART ONE

NEGATIVE FREEDOM

CHAPTER 1

ON NEGATIVE FREEDOM

Probably the most intuitive of all the meanings of the word "freedom" is the absence of coercion. I am free insofar as there is no one else to hinder or stop me from doing what I want to do and, most certainly, if no one forces me to do something I do not want to do. The presence of someone sitting next to me on a bench might prevent me from spreading out all of my belongings on it. He might force me not to light up a cigarette, saying it would be bad for his health, or that there is a no-smoking rule. He might even threaten to call the police and have me prosecuted. I would be subject to an even greater degree of coercion if someone not only prevented me from smoking in his presence but also made me do something else, such as read hefty books on smoking's harmfulness, or drink milk and take medications.

This sense of freedom is usually referred to as "negative" freedom and is so elementary that it would seem to need no further justification. Though many people fear this kind of freedom, and are happy to relinquish some if not most of it, no one can honestly say that they no longer require some domain where they are free do what they want; that what they really desire is to be coerced by others. Throughout history's innumerable struggles for freedom, it would be absurd to imagine anyone fighting for coercion as coercion; that is, with the clear and conscious intention of being seriously and systematically constrained by others. We all agree that being coerced is such an unpleasant experience that wanting it for ourselves would go against human nature. We can also agree that, just as the air we breathe is essential to us so, too, is a certain degree of freedom necessary for our natural development (even if sometimes we are more than ready to deny this to others).

The key issues concern the amount of freedom we actually want and which criteria we will use to distribute this free space. No irrefutable rule has been established yet. Perhaps the problem of distribution (to which we will return in detail later) has become even more engaging than freedom itself. Sometimes we might not be satisfied with the extent of our freedom, not because it is small in the objective sense, but because we consider it insufficient for our purposes and ambitions, or less than the amount others enjoy. Rarely are we sufficiently pleased with what we have to abandon attempts at improving or revising the criteria for its distribution.

Those who defend negative freedom agree that societies face destruction from uncontrollable conflicts in the absence of clear, stable criteria outlining how freedom is apportioned. But attempting to define such principles generates a far more profound problem than one of purely technical difficulties.

Our subjective sense of freedom conflicts fundamentally with any generally applicable principle about how it can be distributed. Negative freedom is always subjective because it applies to individuals. If we need a free space to live, just as we need air to breathe, then we necessarily bring freedom into the subjective realm. That we might make use of our freedom for the well-being of others, or mankind's happiness, is irrelevant. We may indeed use our freedom in that way, but even if we do not, it does not follow that our degree of freedom should be reduced. On the other hand, the rule of distribution should be adopted as an objective principle, independent of the individual's intentions. If we assume that everyone is given a certain degree of negative freedom as a birthright, then establishing rules for its distribution would be tantamount to setting up a social and political constitution.

A necessary tension exists between both of these elements and perspectives. The individual is driven by his own ego to defend his own interests. Society institutes a legal framework to coordinate all those individual egos and, like all systemic undertakings, this becomes an end in itself with no regard for individual preferences or needs.

But once we start building a system of distribution, we are in for more trouble. We might conclude that freedom is not as important a value as its regulation. If someone believes that negative freedom should be equally distributed (granting everybody the same amount) such a person places equality over and above freedom, and thus his sociopolitical system will take away certain freedoms from some people and give them to others. This may make his egalitarian system more restrictive to a particular part of society, thereby undermining its original mission of freedom. If someone else says that freedom should be distributed in accordance with justice, then he makes justice the supreme value. If it is distributed according to a given community's moral values, or in accordance with human nature, then either that community's well-being, or humanity's welfare, becomes the supreme value.

If, however, freedom's regulating principles are not such philosophically loaded notions but merely the product of political negotiations, then we are faced with a different but no less serious problem. Rules generated to serve the interests of those in power will hold only for as long as those egoistic desires are satisfied. But they might not necessarily last forever. Human self-interests are not obliged to observe any rules at all; they are far more likely to take control of them. In that instance, rules lose their inviolability because instead of regulating those self-interests, they become the product of them. Bending the law has been characteristic of all political systems from monarchy, to oligarchy, to democracy. Our current age of democracy is nourished by a belief that is as boastful as it is self-contradictory. It claims that democratic laws are both stable and responsive to people's needs, more resistant than ever to arbitrary power, and more in tune with the new aspirations of our changing times. These claims are irreconcilable: democratic laws are far from stable and not at all resistant to arbitrary power.

The democratic system hopelessly confuses the self-interested aspect of freedom with the law's supposed objectivity and often blends the two together. An individual might assume that his self-interests are restricted by rules not of his own making. However, a democratic majority, an ideologically powerful party, or an interest group that effectively influences the legislature can all pursue their self-interests and fashion the rules concerning how freedom is apportioned. This not only creates a serious constitutional problem of how a democracy secures the fair distribution of liberties, it also creates a linguistic problem. Once one particular group's freedom is confused with the legal framework of freedom, then the language of freedom is likely to become mendacious. And this is what has happened over recent decades in the Western world.

Various interest groups have hijacked freedom and have made the success of their crusades their sole criterion. These groups have somehow managed to convince public opinion–or, more often, the ruling elites–that they pave the way for greater democracy by opening up more free space for hitherto marginalized groups. Identity politics, supported by ethnic studies and so-called gender studies, are cases in point. Whether their powerful effect upon educational institutions and legal systems has resulted in greater democratization is debatable. What cannot be doubted, however, is that they have greatly restricted liberties in practically every area of life, including free speech, free inquiry, and free thought. Additionally, contrary to obvious facts, their successes are generally officially sanctioned by legislatures and courts and presented as victories for freedom. The situation has become so pathological that there is practically no external body left that can question conclusively the constitutional dubiousness of limiting basic liberties and discredit the mendacity of the language in which it is described.

CHAPTER 2

THE WRETCHED WORLD OF ABSOLUTE FREEDOM

Negative freedom can best be understood as a sterile laboratory environment. Let us try to depict what life would be like if we could enjoy the full measure of freedom, without the need to negotiate its limits with anyone else. Such a world has a fictional portrayal: Robinson Crusoe's desert island. Having survived a shipwreck, Crusoe was not disturbed by anyone. No one prohibited him from doing what he wanted, nor ordered him to do anything. Of course, such a world is completely unrealistic or only rarely encountered (serendipitously, if at all) by few individuals.

Let us take a closer look at Robinson Crusoe's situation and determine how it might indeed be desirable. One doesn't have to think too hard to realize that the human mind doesn't often long for absolute freedom. This kind of freedom is not the same kind of desirable goal as, for instance, wealth or power, which can seem limitless in people's imagination and aspirations, even if their boundless accrual might be unrealistic. We want to have greater riches and power, far more than is either attainable or enjoyed by others who have done better for themselves. We want to be richer than John Rockefeller or Bill Gates, more powerful than absolute monarchs or even, in other respects, Harry Potter. Even if such dreams are hatched in the harmless world of fantasy or fairy tales, the very fact of their ubiquity and persistence says something both about our deeply held attitudes towards these goals and about the goals themselves. Yet hardly anyone would want to have Robinson Crusoe's degree of freedom. We might imagine solitary life on a deserted island as a potential short vacation, an occasional rest far away from the hubbub of civilization. We would never think of it with a mixture of craving and regret, as a destiny to be devoutly wished for, yet utterly unattainable and beyond our reach. Being marooned on a deserted island, in absolute freedom, would be more like a nightmare that we shake off with relief once we waken. Daniel Defoe's protagonist was depressed when he realized he was all alone on an uninhabited island. He certainly did not experience the exhilaration he might have felt if instead fate had made him a rich man or a powerful prince.

Absolute negative freedom is therefore not only unreal, but there is no need for it—and not just in the sense that immeasurable riches or excessive power are unnecessary. We certainly have no need for either because, typically, they exceed human nature's moral potential as well as our ability to use them sensibly. We do not require absolute freedom because it runs counter to human nature, so much so that the prospect of having it fills us with dread. We must surely realize that limits to our negative freedom are indispensable. We might be indignant when someone takes away part of our freedom, imposes prohibitions, or sets down orders that we must obey; but the prospect of living in a world devoid of such restrictions would fill us with anxiety. We might not exactly know why we need these restrictions; we would have to stop and think it over, and perhaps we would not all reach the same conclusion. Nonetheless, we would all immediately and unquestionably realize that we could not live without them.

We might claim that what troubled Robinson Crusoe was not so much the absolute negative freedom that suddenly befell him, but rather his loneliness. But absolute freedom is loneliness. If there is no one to enter my existence, no one to react or relate to my words and actions, then in point of fact I am entirely on my own, free to do anything I like, or nothing at all. Absolute freedom must always be accompanied by an extremely painful existential experiment consisting of severing off all of our commitments to others and removing them from beyond the limits of our existence.

We would probably feel a similar fear at the prospect of our freedom being radically deprived; for instance, if we were imprisoned. We dread the idea of life in prison and consider such a condition contrary to our elementary existential needs. Prison is quite rightly used as a place of punishment, not as a place for moral advancement. Understandably, attempts at making prison such a place have rarely been successful since the unnatural conditions of prison life cannot readily be turned into a means of preparing individuals for being in their natural condition, namely life in the company of others.

What is extraordinary is that the fear of prison has a lot in common with the fear of absolute freedom. Both situations are extreme. In both cases, we are condemned to total, unbearable isolation: in the former, on the grounds of a judge's verdict; in the latter, by random chance or by choice. In certain respects, deprivation of freedom and absolute freedom overlap. Their external conditions are diametrically different, but their existential situations are similar. Robinson Crusoe felt as if he were in prison not only because he could not leave the island but also because, like a prisoner, he was condemned to his own company. We can do very few of the things we want to do in prison, while there is no one to stop us from doing anything on a desert island. Yet, despite this significant disparity, it does not alter the overriding experience of having life's natural rhythm fundamentally disturbed. Some people might prefer being in jail; some might not be bothered by absolute solitude. The general, well-grounded consensus is, however, that such attitudes are anomalous.

Take, for instance, the simplest example of negative liberty: freedom of speech. The point of freedom of speech is not about prohibiting opposition to what someone says, but rather providing a space in which others can hear and respond to what they have to say. Supporters of free speech have complained that certain laws, institutions, and customs often prevent us from saying what we want. But it is not hard to see that some forms of external pressure (while sometimes annoying) are what make this liberty so attractive and worth striving for. The absence of such pressure renders a statement ineffectual, thereby making it socially redundant. An individual who finds himself in a world where freedom of speech is absolute would be reminiscent of Robinson Crusoe yelling out his opinions on the beach of his island, or a prisoner addressing the empty walls of his cell.

Absolute negative freedom is not a rational aspiration because for all practical purposes it is beyond our grasp and, above all, because it comes dangerously close to its exact opposite. This is not true of other aspirations. Striving for and accumulating great wealth would not lead us into a condition similar to that of a pauper; nor would we resemble the powerless if we gained exorbitant power (although it could give rise to a variety of contradictions). By its very nature, negative freedom must be limited, otherwise it would result in unwanted consequences that, paradoxically, we would choose freedom to avoid.

CHAPTER 3

MAXIMUM FREEDOM

MANKIND'S NATURAL CONDITION

Since the world of absolute freedom is never a reality to anyone save Robinson Crusoe, one has to look for a more realistic option. A world of maximum freedom would be such an option. In such a society, all individuals have as much freedom as possible, their only limitation being the greatest possible freedom of others. This is, obviously, a purely theoretical construct, a daring thought experiment that imagines a world from which all obstacles to freedom have been removed. Philosophers have found this idea intellectually tempting and called it "the state of nature" or "the natural condition of mankind."

Why consider "the state of nature" only to imagine a world that does not exist? The answer is well-known. By framing a hypothetical reality of maximum freedom, we can see more clearly how many liberties have been taken away from us in the real world. Having discovered that, we can then reflect upon how to recover much of this lost freedom by abolishing the unnecessary limitations that have been created over time. Ultimately, this thought experiment typically serves as a vehicle for the thorough, even radical, reform of political structures.

Influential as it is, this reform strategy can be powerfully counterargued primarily because of the controversial theoretical assumptions underpinning the concept of mankind's natural condition. Two constitutive principles have to be assumed for the world of maximum freedom to exist, and each has provoked serious doubts.

The first such principle holds that in the natural condition people are conceived as individuals, not as social beings. Communities such as families (if they exist) are considered secondary, often provisional, and temporary so as not to encroach on the liberty of individuals. These communities can be relatively easily dissolved or changed depending on the self-interests and desires of the people within them. Perhaps the most radical version of individualism can be found in the work of Rousseau, who claimed that individuals living in the state of nature were self-contained, pre-moral beings, motivated by the simplest and most natural desires. "If we consider man just as he must have come from the hands of nature," he wrote, "we behold in him an animal weaker than some, and less agile than others; but, taking him all round, the most advantageously organized of any. I see him satisfying his hunger at the first oak, and slaking his thirst at the first brook; finding his bed at the foot of the tree which afforded him a repast; and, with that, all his wants supplied."[1]

In the natural condition's second organizing principle, all people are equal; their aspirations and goals are of equal value, and in this respect no individual is privileged. Hobbes wrote of physical and intellectual equality among people in the state of nature. "As to the strength of body," he wrote, "the weakest has strength enough to kill the strongest, either by secret machination or by confederacy with others, that are in the same danger with himself." Hobbes also believed men were equal intellectually: "For Prudence, is but Experience; which equall time, equally bestowes on all men, in those things they equally apply themselves unto." He continued: "That which may perhaps make such equality incredible, is but a vain conceipt of ones owne wisdome, which almost all men think they have in a greater degree than the Vulgar; that is, than all men but themselves, and a few others, whom by Fame, or for concurring with themselves, they approve."[2]

Both principles–the individualistic concept of society and the natural equality of all people—are far from self-evident. Even less radical forms than those of Rousseau and Hobbes do not impose themselves irresistibly on our minds; nor do we perceive them as particularly attractive ways to secure our freedom. They may indeed constitute a more realistic world than Robinson Crusoe's, but this world is still quite removed from the conditions in which most of us would want to see ourselves.

Unpleasant as this world might seem, it does not make it any less compelling. Those who put forward the state-of-nature theory argued that compromising these two assumptions—allowing a more organic concept of society and rejecting equality as key to human nature and as a political norm—would seriously limit liberty's original state and, consequently, would weaken liberty's role in the political systems built around it.

But a price would have to be paid. If absolute freedom made an individual feel miserable, living in such a world would no doubt make him less lonely since he would interact with others. Still, human interaction would have to be cold, impersonal, and formal to a degree that most would find hard to bear. The two constitutive principles would force human nature into a framework that most would rather avoid.

Moreover, it is not at all obvious that it would be a price worth paying. In the institutional constructs that emerge after people have left the state of nature, the initial plan to give every individual an equal share of freedom has to be significantly modified. Individualism is there, as is egalitarianism, but the amount of freedom accorded to each individual drastically decreases. Neither Hobbes's bureaucratic state, Rousseau's republicanism, or Locke's private property-based contractarianism retained much of the original state of maximum freedom. Indeed, one may wonder why all this fuss about natural liberty if it lead to the creation of a state in which there was so little left of it. In the political systems of Burke or Hegel—both radically opposed to the state-of-nature theory—there was often more freedom than in those of Hobbes, Rousseau, or Locke. Moreover, in Burke's and Hegel's societies, loneliness was eliminated as human existence acquired a social dimension, with no particular loss of liberty.

The theorists, it should be added, were of two minds about the state of nature. On the one hand, it was conceived as an essentially unsustainable situation that people departed from by building political institutions. Usually, a daunting sense of insecurity motivated people to create some kind of political covenant or contract that protected them from one another by establishing a political body strong enough to enforce rules of cooperation.

These philosophers did not consider loneliness and human happiness a major problem. Somehow, it was assumed that if individualism was sufficiently developed, it could provide people with goals that would counterbalance the absence of communal life and non-individualistic, non-contractual obligations. More importantly, within this theoretical framework, the problem of loneliness would not arise because the assumption that individuals were self-contained and thus self-sufficient beings invalidated it. Only Rousseau noticed that living in a modern society made us wretched by depriving us of life's original simple authenticity. Yet his answer to this defect—which combined sentimentalism with democracy, the cult of authenticity with inculcating civic virtues, individualism with communitarianism—though remarkably influential, was deeply problematic.

On the other hand, it is therefore not surprising that, as unsustainable as the state of nature was, theorists could not hide their sympathy and desire to preserve some of its attractive features. The best-known example was Locke's state of nature which was depicted in such lively colors that the reader might wonder why, having been so beneficial, it had to disappear and be suddenly and somewhat unexpectedly transformed into a gruesome state of war. But even in a developed political society, where individuals managed to retain their self-contained status, the state of nature could somehow shine through and be observed with satisfaction.

There were, of course, darker pictures of the natural condition, the most vivid being those painted by Hobbes. He claimed that the violence and mutual distrust prevalent in the state of nature never disappeared, no matter how strong society was or how powerful the state's law enforcement.

The dark side of nature comes to the fore in our lives when we lock our houses before going on a journey, or lock our chests when leaving the house in the sole care of servants and children. But our rootedness in the state of nature is not only about distrust and a sense of insecurity. Hobbes' individuals gave up a lot of their freedom for security, but never really forgot that state-imposed political barriers, laws, and other constraints were artificial constructs. Deep down, they were still free and equal individuals, not too dissimilar from those one could imagine living their "solitary, poor, nasty, brutish, and short" lives in the state of nature.[3]

Although we cannot say that mankind's natural condition provided a political blueprint, some of its features were often found attractive or, by the same token, unavoidable–including the two constitutive principles which, being "natural," acquired a special importance. While it was true that existing political structures required reform, having become deformed irreparably over the course of time, it was also quite understandable that what had initially been a thought experiment began to be either partially or wholly treated as a viable political model that potentially could be created. After all, the view of society comprised of equal individuals did not lose its validity, either in the state of nature or once state institutions had been constructed.

Thus, from the beginning, there was an ambiguity about the way the state of nature was both conceived and perceived. On the one hand, it was something people moved away from; on the other hand, if modified, it was something people could consider moving towards. It belonged to a hypothetical beginning, but it could also stimulate thinking about a hypothetical end. It could be associated with the past, and also with the future.

SOCIETY AS A DEPARTMENT STORE

This confusing attitude towards mankind's natural condition became most visible in libertarianism; that is, in the theories which (to put it somewhat crudely) refused to conclude that the state-of-nature hypothesis necessitated a strong government. Instead, these theories contended that initial freedom could be sustained with a minimal state, or even with no state at all. They advocated for a society with maximum diversity, plurality, tolerance, and few to no restrictions, in which every group or individual was allowed to pursue their own aims.

Libertarianism may be regarded as an episodic offshoot in the history of political theory, but today's prevailing ideological jargon of liberal democracy reflects some of its main tenets. The lavish use of such words as "diversity," "pluralism," and "tolerance" point to a political order that provides maximum freedom for all. Whether today's liberal democratic theories and ideologies are somehow indebted to the state-of-nature concept is an interesting problem for an historian of political ideas, but of minor importance in this context. What is significant is that they all subscribe emphatically to the same principles: that society consists of individuals; that individuals are equal in how they define themselves; and that an individual's or group's freedom is limited only by that of others.

Indulging in political fantasies, one could say that this kind of ideal society would be somewhere in which there was room for every human desire and life plan. A place where all occupations and aspirations were allowed, religions and non-religions coexisted, where all groups, associations, parties, and clubs could peacefully pursue their goals, uninhibited either by minute legal regulations or by other groups, associations, parties, or clubs, so long as they did not interfere with the rules of cooperation and did not impose their views on others. It is a society of Christians, Muslims, Buddhists, and atheists; heterosexuals, homosexuals, innumerable genders, nationalities, and ethnic backgrounds; conservatives, liberals, socialists, anarchists, communists, and those with other political beliefs; pornographers, priests, hedonists, and moral ascetics—all of whom respect a common set of rules. Greater superiority or privilege is not given to any one group simply because it is larger than the others. Metaphorically speaking, one could say that such a society resembles a department store in which everything is offered, everyone can find what they want, no one feels underserved, one can change one's preferences, and even the most selective desires can be satisfied.

Even in less radical versions, this view of society meets with an obvious counterargument, similar to that which was raised against the state of nature: it mixes two worlds. On the one hand, it is the blueprint for a good society organized on the state-of-nature's principles of equality and individualism. On the other, this society is populated by individuals and groups whose identities have evolved in very different environments over the course of history. As Christians, Muslims, socialists, nationalists, or anarchists, we anchor ourselves (sometimes very closely) to certain historical narratives as well as to moral traditions and many other formative philosophical conditions and contingencies that influence our perception of the world. One simply cannot put a Christian, a Muslim, a socialist, and a conservative into an individualistic/egalitarian framework and expect them to be Christian, Muslim, socialist, or conservative in the standard sense of the word. Similarly, being born into this individualistic/ egalitarian social framework, one cannot become a Christian, a Muslim, a socialist, or a conservative in the sense that these identities have always been understood, while at the same time be a loyal and dedicated member of a libertarian society.

Libertarians and other radical pluralists seem to ignore this problem and maintain faith in its practicality. They sincerely believe a system of maximum liberty and diversity should become a sort of utopia that ignites a fire in people's imagination and pushes them to seek a better world (as the ideology of communism once did), though this time such enthusiasm would be for an unquestionably good cause. How can a system that promises maximum freedom for each and every person be questioned? Yet the very same theorists who cherish such high hopes also express disappointment at this plan's meager results because the program to make society infinitely open and unperturbed by government has never really taken off.

It is easy to see why it has not. The program crumbles because it attempts to square the circle. Two loyalties—one particular to one's own community, the other to an infinitely open system–cannot be reconciled. Each community has a different understanding and evaluation of society's values. Besides, each has differing notions of freedom and human nature as well as divergent (sometimes irreconcilable) notions about man's destiny and what constitutes good political order. For example, freedom for Christians has always been interpreted in a way liberals found unacceptable, and vice versa. Fundamental differences can be seen by comparing Pope Leo XIII's *Rerum Novarum* with John Stuart Mill's plea for liberty or read the reactions of liberals and libertarians to Pope John Paul II's encyclicals.[4] The same goes for Muslims, communists, nationalists, and many others. No wonder a utopia built on diversity has never really exhilarated mankind's imagination and is unlikely to do so in the future.

The libertarian world's most misleading aspect has been the spatial representation that its description seems to suggest. This goes back, obviously, to the concept of negative freedom (so dear to all libertarians) which is also conceived as a space free from coercion. We visualize libertarian society as an even larger space, so large that it can provide all groups and individuals with their own territories in which each can do what they want, while government's role is to ensure that those territorial borders are respected. Or, to use a different picture, we can imagine libertarian society as a gigantic department store, where people can move freely through every conceivable department whenever they want, in pursuit of the goods they wish to have.

But these spatial associations are deceitful. A society is a space, to be sure, but certainly not an infinite one, and there are areas that cannot be separated in a spatial or quasi-spatial way. Laws, culture, education, customs, traditions, and many other areas cannot be turned into separate departments (or sections within departments) as in a large store. They are all meant to be inscribed into society's governing regulations and, as such, are fundamentally important to both government and each group that wants to have an impact on how the entire system works. Communities and individuals compete with one another not only (or even primarily) for the size of their sovereign territory, but for the power to adapt those rules to their own interests. To think that they will all renounce this competition and be satisfied solely with their territorial security not only shows complete political ignorance but also misunderstands the nonspatial, indivisible character of many of society's constituent factors.

One can see it most clearly in those parts of the real world that are dominated by the ideology of multiculturalism, which today means practically all of Western civilization. Multiculturalism has appeared as a result of spontaneous tendencies in liberal democratic societies not usually associated with libertarianism—a theory often regarded as the radical, political fantasy of a few doctrinaire minds with a profound, almost obsessive aversion to government. This rather dismissive depiction of libertarianism may be generally accurate, but the very notion that society should be made more spacious and inclusive shows some significant affinity between multiculturalism and liberalism/libertarianism.

What puts multiculturalism at odds with libertarianism, however, is that governments are not minimal in present-day multicultural societies, as they should be according to libertarian precepts. In fact, current governments are quite powerful and increasingly intrusive, regulating ever more aspects of social life, while deafening propaganda supports this social engineering. One can rightly say that there is no other way a multicultural society (or any other society built of separate blocks) can be sustained but through governmental interference, as well as incessant propaganda justifying this interference to conceal the cracks in the entire political edifice. Libertarians are no exception to this. Certainly, the libertarian remedy has never been tried but, had it been, it would have ended up being an enormous government-based machine for social engineering and systemic brainwashing, just as multicultural politics have become.

All political projects that neglect human nature and disregard the lessons drawn from centuries of political experience have to compensate for their lack of realism by a disproportionately high degree of intervention in both the social fabric and in human minds. It often means annexing those areas of human existence in which negative freedom typically expresses itself and is most needed, such as education, rulemaking, culture, thinking, social practices, and language. This act of annexation is presented–falsely, let me hasten to add–as restricted to, and conducted in, the level of cooperation between communities, groups, and cultures, not within them. Being more procedural than substantive, it therefore does not limit the freedom that each community, group, or culture has in itself or by itself.

One can see this false claim in the phenomenon of political correctness which has been defended precisely as an attempt to guarantee only cooperation among groups, without touching those groups' identities. Admittedly, this argument has been persuasive, since political correctness has spread by leaps and bounds across the Western world, and proclamations of its coming demise have been premature. But the overall effects of political correctness have been disastrous for freedom, as well as for other basic ideas such as beauty, goodness, and truth.

THE TYRANNY OF LIBERALISM

Let me repeat, a fundamental flaw in the libertarian/multicultural model is its division into two levels: one for rules of cooperation that are applied to the entire society; another for particular creeds or beliefs that are supposedly at the sole disposal of each group or community. This model comes with two accompanying claims: first, that these two levels can be kept separate; second, that the level of cooperation may be somehow minimal and relatively easy to accept by all members of society.

There are only two groups for whom this model could be acceptable. The first we usually call liberals/libertarians. They are in the opportune situation of being able to identify with both levels–the rules that govern the entire pluralistic libertarian and/or multicultural society, and those that govern their own community. In fact, the entire society is their own community, and there is no need for them to enclose themselves inside a separate liberal territory. The rules that would have kept this territory integral are the same as those that the whole of society has to respect.

This, of course, gives them a privileged position. Not only are they better off in the sense that they are spared a possible conflict between two loyalties, but they become *de facto* rulers, educators, ideologues, guardians, and censors for all members of society. They control the language of public discourse, create the cultural environment, and are judges in formal and informal tribunals that pronounce verdicts about what is and is not admissible within society's governing rules.

The second group consists of those individuals and groups who have willingly given up their own particular views or have modified them so much that they are ready to acknowledge the general principles of negative freedom as morally superior. Anything in their particular views that clashes with those principles is rejected, suspended, or made harmless. Sometimes these concessions are found in doctrines or in practice; sometimes they may result from sheer opportunism to accommodate themselves to social pressure, masked by the obscure rhetoric of catching up with modernity.

Some movements within Christianity are perhaps the most notorious examples. Lured by the alleged virtue of open-mindedness, they adapt their language and thoughts to liberal ideology, believing that by doing so they pay very little price as Christians and gain a respectable position in a liberal/multicultural society. There are Christians who instead of opposing abortion do their best to condone it theologically. There are also Christians (probably the same ones) who instead of condemning homosexual acts as sinful and unnatural, call for the recognition of the right of homosexuals to marry and adopt children. All this in the belief that the rules of "open society," which (as they were made to accept for no good reason) must include the rights to abortion and same-sex marriage, are politically superior to the moral teachings of Christianity.

These two groups are, upon reflection, one group. Much as one would like to find something in the second group (the "open Christians") that would make a difference and add to society's plurality by expanding its political and philosophical spectrum, one cannot really detect any particular mark distinguishing them from liberals and multiculturalists.

The initial plan to have general liberal principles applied across society to secure equal freedom for everybody had to fail because it was either ill-conceived or fraudulent. What allegedly served negative freedom was not about freedom at all. The most notorious examples of the liberties gained in Western societies in recent decades–namely, the public use of vulgar language, public media's broadcasting of explicit sex and violence, euthanasia, same-sex marriage and the right for homosexuals to adopt children, almost unlimited rights to abortion, including for underage girls without the knowledge of their parents–imply far more than just granting more freedom to particular individuals or groups.

Let us repeat, these changes have not been about freedom but about fundamental ideas of good and evil, of life and death. One can hardly accept the argument that euthanasia is good because it extends an individual's scope of freedom: those who accept it have access to it; those who reject it morally are not be forced to do so. Likewise, one cannot argue that pornography is acceptable on the grounds that it enlarges an individual's free choice without enforcing it on those who morally object to it.

One can find some such argument in the joint declaration made by a group of influential American philosophers–John Rawls, Judith Jarvis Thomson, Robert Nozick, Ronald Dworkin, T.M. Scanlon, and Thomas Nagel–who acted as *amicus curiae* in a 1996 ruling by the Supreme Court of the United States on a type of euthanasia known as "assisted suicide."[5] One can reconstruct their argument as follows: there are situations of fundamental importance for human life, such as marriage, birth, death, procreation, religion, and values, about which people have widely divergent moral and philosophical opinions but through which they define the ultimate meaning of life. Governments and legislators should leave such matters for individuals to decide according to their conscience and beliefs, and refrain from using the law to authoritatively and arbitrarily define the ultimate meaning of life for society as a whole. Such decisions should be made philosophically, derived from an individual person's dignity and autonomy, and protected by the liberties guaranteed by the United States Constitution.

This argument is spurious. Leaving the questions of abortion, marriage, or euthanasia for individuals to decide is in itself a decision that dramatically changes society, a decision comparable to a revolution. The judges and legislators who argue as such are not motivated by self-restraint with the intention to live and let live. On the contrary, they act like revolutionaries who with one signature achieve what radicals of yore could not have gained using arms and shedding blood. Once such a law is in force, it not only implies legal admissibility, but also moral acceptance of such practices. After all, one cannot live in a society in which the law allows something that is morally reprehensible. Therefore, soon after such a law is passed, new laws are introduced to make moral opposition to this law more difficult and legally risky. People who oppose these practices on moral grounds are soon qualified as representing a type of backwardness, bigotry, and authoritarianism that cannot be accepted in a society that pushed forward the limits of liberty and opened the way for a better future. Their assertions are first dismissed as profoundly incorrect, and then outlawed. For example, those who publicly criticize abortion or homosexual marriage are, in some countries such as France, not only ostracized or bullied but also can be punished by law on the grounds that those criticisms assault both the legal system and human rights.

Legal decisions to equalize how "the meaning of life" is interpreted (allowing all to exist side by side), have turned into a powerful crusade to hunt down the allegedly old, incorrect rights and enforce the new, correct ones. Of late, the crusaders have succeeded in getting hold of major institutions and other instruments of power.

It is symptomatic of how the officially permitted attitude to abortion has changed over the years since it was originally legalized. First it was called the choice of a lesser evil, then a somewhat shameful but routine operation, then a human right (or rather a woman's right), and finally one of the European values that symbolizes progress and enlightenment. Together with these changes, there has emerged an entire industry to legitimize, propagate, and finally export abortion through education (usually indistinguishable from indoctrination), mass media, and popular culture–all affecting the public space and much of the population's moral imagination. Some governments, such as Canada's, have openly declared that "sexual reproductive rights and the right to safe and accessible abortions [...] are at the core of our foreign policy."[6] International organizations, including the European Commission, started exporting it to other continents through more or less legally dubious means.[7] To say that one can divide Europe along libertarian/multicultural lines into various moral territories with different attitudes towards abortion, family, or education sounds like a pathetic *naïveté* or an offense to one's intelligence.

In matters of this kind, there are no exclusively individual decisions. What happened with the issue of abortion was repeated with same-sex marriage, pornography, and other elements of the moral revolution. Permitting the distribution of pornography not only sanctioned the business socially but, by shifting the boundaries of admissibility, also dramatically changed Western civilization's moral and aesthetic sensibilities. The courts' decisions had a colossal impact upon societies and had nothing to do with individual interpretations of the ultimate meaning of existence. The choice was made for millions of people by a few judges or hundreds of legislators from assorted chambers.

All rulings that courts make about matters of life and death are moral judgments, yet the concepts of good and evil are absent. To say that such rulings are only legal and not moral, is not true. When judges or parliamentarians legalize certain actions, they both legitimize and absolve them of their prior moral opprobrium. Similarly, when legislators prohibit certain actions, they directly (or indirectly) stigmatize them as being morally bad. Legalizing abortion made it not only morally neutral, but soon morally acceptable, and then morally commendable. Prohibiting capital punishment made it legally inadmissible, but also morally wrong.

Using the argument of individuals' right to negative freedom to justify such legal decisions is therefore disingenuous. In most cases, these decisions have been made with the deliberate intention of changing society's moral fabric, and the legal reasonings about individual freedoms and "the meaning of life" serve only as efficient tools with which to do so. This dishonesty shows itself in the glaringly disproportionate scale of the legal arguments compared to the effects of the courts' decisions. The legal arguments are usually modest, filled with qualifications, defensive, ostentatiously noncommittal in moral, metaphysical, and religious matters, full of pro-freedom rhetoric, abstract, and cleverly decorated with legal references to give them a dryly principled character. One can hardly believe that these arguments could (and sometimes have) shaken society's foundations, doing away with institutions such as marriage that have existed since time immemorial. The judges and the parliamentarians (not to mention the philosophers that provided the intellectual groundwork for these decisions) all seem serenely untroubled by the revolution that they have set in motion, pretending to have simply provided a formal solution to an interesting intellectual problem.

HUMAN RIGHTS AND THE STATE OF NATURE

The confusion surrounding the concept of the state of nature has led some theorists and politicians, as well as much of the population, to believe they can live in the modern world yet somehow retain the blessings of the state of nature. Although their political language no longer uses or makes indirect reference to the concept itself, philosophically the origin of this perception is clear. Peculiar as this belief may be, it has nevertheless become most seductive. Increasing numbers of people believe that they can somehow temporarily, or even permanently, suspend some of their obligations to the society in which they live, yet still profit from its institutions. To put it differently, they believe they can jump from the current political system into some kind of pre-political freedom, then jump back into the real world again.

Nowhere is this confusion of what is natural and what has come from civilization more visible than in the concept of human rights–a concept which has acquired the status of a political religion in the Western world over the past few decades. From the outset, however, there has been an inherent ambiguity in the language of rights. Originally, each individual in the state of nature was said to possess an unlimited scope of freedom because, first, there was no external authority to regulate it by imposing limits and restrictions and, second, because people were deemed essentially equal. This, as we know from Hobbes's story and other accounts, created conflicts between individuals to which the only solution was to give up a lot of rights and establish a state to provide order and protection. But whatever the story's later chapters, no one doubted that, in the state of nature, everyone was free to make an infinite number of claims. "Naturally," as Hobbes wrote, "man has right to everything."[8]

It was hoped however that some of these claims, primarily the basic ones, could be carried over into a political society–for instance, a claim to property, to life, or to living in peace. Since they came from the state of nature they were called "natural," meaning pre-political and pre-institutional, independent of any political and legal arrangements, and irrevocable by any authority. At the same time, however, a significant shift of meaning occurred. When Hobbes said that man in the natural condition had an infinite number of rights, he meant that man was able to make an infinite number of claims, not that he had the right to obtain them. However, once this "right" was carried over into a political society, it ceased to be merely a claim but a "right" in a new sense–that is, a justifiable demand that this claim could be satisfied.

This initial confusion surrounding the concept of rights continues to this today and is likely to continue henceforth. These rights were never really natural. What made them seem "natural" was their obscure origin in a hypothetical reality, one where they were simply the demands and expectations of individuals who were unprotected by any civilization, laws, or political structures, and who had but a slim chance and no guarantee of their fulfillment. To have such a guarantee, a political and civilizational system had to be created that would use its resources and instruments to have these expectations and demands implemented. But once such a system appeared, those rights became purely artificial and fully dependent on the new system's efficiency.

The word "natural" soon fell out of use and new adjectives started to be employed, of which the best known was "inalienable." But the confusion remained the same. Some alleged claims in the pre-political, abstract space–unsubstantiated by any solid arguments–were taken over by political groups and incorporated into the laws and institutions of real political systems that pledged to fulfill them. These claims/rights were called inalienable precisely because they were believed to come from some mysterious pre-political, even pre-moral, world independent of actual conventions, which was rather bizarre because these rights were derived solely from real countries' existing laws and institutions.

Let us take the best-known example in Western political history. While one can find more or less convincing, or at least rational, arguments that "all men are created equal," in no way can one justify a statement that all men "are endowed by their Creator with certain unalienable Rights [...] among these [...] Life, Liberty and the pursuit of Happiness."[9] There is nothing in the Christian religion that would even indirectly supply grounds for such an outlandish contention, nor is there anything of the kind in the history of philosophy. Certainly, this is not a Cartesian statement that, freed of particularities, the mind grasps clearly and distinctly (*clare ac distincte*) as being true; nor is it an analytic proposition that could be regarded as being true on account of its self-evidence.

Yet the authors of this famous document stated clearly: "We hold these truths to be self-evident."[10] Who held these truths to be self-evident? The only explanation could be that this was a foundational statement expressing the decision of the framers of a new state to treat the idea of inalienable rights as a basic philosophical assumption. Additionally, that assumption was binding for all future generations, all institutions had to respect it, and it had to be acknowledged by all men as the core of their political creed. But this meant that American citizens (as well as those from other countries which at a certain point of their development made similar decisions) were henceforth entitled to make extremely strong claims with no regard to any obligations to the state, their community, or even their fellow citizens. Such obligations were always weaker because they came after a political system had been founded, while the rights had existed logically and philosophically prior to any legal, moral, or political opinions. That opened the way for the peculiar conviction, never openly articulated but deeply ingrained in people's behavior, that one could have the best of two worlds; that is, that one could move from the state of nature, where rights had their grounding, to civilization which had the instruments to fulfill them.

It is therefore not surprising that this view, which is confusing in itself, created even more confusion in its consequences. Perhaps the most momentous one was the effect on the role of the state. There were at least three not particularly harmonious versions of this role. The first version held that natural or inalienable rights served as protection from primarily governmental abuses of power because government was usually unaccountable to anyone but itself and wielded more power than any other agency. Unlawful arrests, notorious miscarriages of justice, confiscations of property, and violence of every kind–these were practices that had to be stopped; implementing rights that both predated and were independent of any power system seemed a perfect legal and moral safeguard.

Fear of the state's arbitrary power has been a permanent trait in political evolution from reforms, revolutions, conflicts, to institution building, although its actual influence on how states function has varied from country to country. The Polish nation, for example, was obsessively apprehensive of political absolutism for many centuries, and was inclined to treat every attempt to revert the state's gradual dismantling as a sinister plan to restore *absolutum dominium*. It paid dearly for this. But the Third of May Constitution of 1791 (the final effort to save the state from decomposition) made it clear that a good, efficient political system must respect people's rights. It stated: "We shall have and preserve the right to personal security, personal freedom, and to real and movable property, observed sacrosanct and intact as they have been enjoyed by all for many ages; and we do solemnly pledge that we shall suffer no change or exception in the law against the property of any man; indeed, our Country's supreme authority and the government it institutes shall make no claims to the property of citizens, on the pretense of *iuria regalia* or on any other grounds, either wholly or in part."[11]

This anti-despotic concept continued to appear in similar texts from the 18th century to the 20th century, including the Universal Declaration of Human Rights. The latter specifically referenced the Second World War's barbarity which brutally deprived people of their life, freedom, and property on a hitherto unprecedented scale.

The second version maintains that the state should protect rights. The classical liberal texts specifically indicate the rights to liberty, property, and security. The United States Declaration of Independence, penned in 1776, mentions explicitly "Safety and Happiness" (this second word looking somewhat puzzling). But the general picture is clear. Society consists of individuals who want to be safe from aggression and lawlessness and are mainly concerned with their property (in the larger sense of the word). They also want to have "Happiness," which probably means a general satisfaction with the system as a whole.

From this description, it is not certain what other duties the state has, but we may safely presume that they must somehow relate to these few explicitly listed rights. But having "Safety and Happiness" can mean infinitely many things, and it is no wonder that as people's expectations rose so did the state's duties. Almost two centuries later, in the 1948 Universal Declaration of Human Rights, one can read about "economic,

social, and cultural" rights, as well as about the rights to "social security."[12]
It may very well be that having all of these rights satisfied increases our
"Safety and Happiness" and that some governments may try to satisfy
them. But, one cannot resist the feeling that when making such demands
on government we long ago left the philosophical territory in which the
whole idea of rights started. There is no abstract pre-political, pre-moral,
or pre-civilizational position that can be used as a basis upon which one
can formulate a demand for cultural rights or the right to social security.
One can, of course, argue that these benefits are important, socially valuable, and morally laudable, and that any government may afford to grant
them to its citizens. But, whatever their value, these benefits certainly have
nothing to do with "self-evident truths," Kantian practical reason, or the
goals we could have enjoyed in the state of nature.

The third version is a radicalized version of the second. It states that
not only is the state entrusted with protecting rights, that is its sole duty.
Failing to discharge this duty deprives the state of legitimacy, thus entitling
citizens to replace it with another one. Although liberal thinkers from
Locke onwards treated this as the ultimate weapon not to be used reck-
lessly, the principle itself was clear. Even the United States Declaration
of Independence reads: "Whenever any Form of Government becomes
destructive of these ends, it is the Right of the People to alter or to abolish it, and to institute new Government, laying its foundation on such
principles and organizing its powers in such form, as to them shall seem
most likely to effect their Safety and Happiness."[13]

Due to many additional qualifications this view was never treated
literally, but rather served as an *ad hoc* justification for revolutionary ventures. But in the 20th century, after the Universal Declaration of Human
Rights was proclaimed, and subsequent international conventions and
agreements were signed confirming the paramount role of human rights,
the view transformed somewhat, even though it still came from the same
intellectual source. Growing numbers of people, organizations, and even
governments began promulgating the idea that respecting human rights

should be regarded as a basic criterion for evaluating political regimes. Those regimes that fell short should be considered somehow illegitimate and be kept outside the community of civilized nations. In the latter half of the 20th century, countries such as Rhodesia and South Africa were ostracized internationally, punished by economic sanctions and threatened with other severe measures.

But this criterion was used selectively. Countries powerful enough to ignore these threats and counterattack in various ways, such as the Soviet Union and Communist China, were not met with harsh reprisals and were spared much of the verbal criticism. In contrast with some American administrations, Western European governments never really used the concept of human rights to antagonize the Soviet Union, preferring some kind of no-nonsense policy that lead to more or less permanent accommodation with the powerful Soviet empire. In point of fact, dissident movements within the USSR were not greeted with much enthusiasm by Western European nations because they were perceived as creating embarrassing obstacles to their policy of accommodation.

This view has had another twist in recent decades, especially in the European Union, but also in other Western countries. Some of the newly created human rights–in particular, those referring to the profoundly moral problems of life and death–have been elevated to being the fundamental criteria of "European values." This has been a rather bizarre move. Both international institutions and sovereign governments have created this moral disorder and then anointed it by giving it a "European" label, although their revolution has been a shameless violation of European moral traditions.

These three versions of the state do not, to say the least, form a harmonious whole. If we imagine the state of mind of an ideal believer in human rights, we might get a not particularly edifying picture. His mind will be permeated by a deep fear of political power, verging on anarchy in its more radical variants, while at the same time sliding into dependency on the state which he will expect to bestow ever more favors, privileges, exemptions, and handouts upon him. Fueling the machinery of the state by multiplying its functions and duties, as well as supplying it with an ideological cover-up, he will easily turn into a rebel, a revolutionary, or a dissident demanding radical reforms and sweeping changes, always eager to dethrone the old leaders and enthrone the new ones. He will see himself as a moralist who brings people peace, mutual respect, and tolerance. Simultaneously, having developed a deep sense of the enemy, he will be tracking down all real and imagined violations of rights, hurling wild accusations and, paradoxically, with every human rights victory, he will wage new wars against an ever-growing number of enemies of human rights, finding new sins, -isms, and -phobias to condemn. Surprisingly, this mind, torn by opposing forces and feeding on irreconcilable ideas, seems unaware of its internal disorder and the impropriety of its reactions.

Due to its philosophical vacuity, the concept of human rights never had, nor could have, any satisfactory justification or larger and deeper intellectual groundwork. Human rights have entered the public arena through declarations and charters—that is, through an arbitrary political act of will that by definition requires no prior rational validation. There has always been a striking disparity between the scarcity of arguments to justify the concept of rights and the tremendous and far-reaching effects they have had on society.

It should be duly noted however that the Universal Declaration of Human Rights contains a kind of justification, which, though appearing as a rather cursory remark in the text, has become widely accepted. It states that all human beings have an inborn dignity that entitles them to rights irrespective of, and prior to, any political or legal arrangement within which they live. In response to this criticism, one could say that those who claim human rights do not willingly and conveniently jump between an abstract, arbitrarily constructed situation and civilization (with all of its instruments that have been laboriously created throughout history) simply because they retain their dignity in both worlds.

This solution has had a spectacular, though somewhat surprising, career.

There is hardly anything in the writings of Hobbes, Locke, Jefferson, or others that would even remotely resemble the argument about dignity. Whatever characteristics they attributed to human nature, dignity was not one of them. Dignity could be found in Kant though; but when he invoked it, he had at his disposal a more densely complex view of human nature than the British, French, and American liberals. The concept itself was, of course, not new; we encounter it in antiquity, for example, in the works of Cicero. The word is the same, but the meaning clearly different. Cicero's formula, "to each the dignity he deserves," (*suam cuique digni- tatem*) carried obvious meritocratic implications, since it suggested that dignity was not distributed equally among people nor was it attributed to an individual merely on the grounds of his being born. Dignity had to be earned and, consequently, could be lost through ignoble acts.

Many centuries later, dignity took a radical departure from its classical version. It became the property of an abstract individual; one with no particular moral achievements to his credit. Nonetheless, the word still sounds impressive—so much so, that when included in doctrines concerning human rights it retains the same aura of nobility that the ancient notion of dignity had.

In fact, the opposite is true. In classical doctrines (supported by common sense) dignity was always about obligations—as the principle *noblesse oblige* unequivocally indicates—but never about rights. Relating dignity to rights was a drastic semantic violation of an important moral category. Today's doctrine—*toutes proportions gardées*—could be compared to the ideology of hereditary aristocrats, who claimed that simply through birth they were entitled to certain liberties and privileges, except that today these have been extended to all human beings and not limited to a single social class.

Just as for aristocrats, who used their alleged dignity to absolve their undignified behavior, today dignity-based rights serve as justification for base activities that no morally sane person can defend. Dignity, in other words, should be about the high and sublime, not the low and vulgar.

How can one preserve dignity when doing undignified things? There is something odiously dissonant when in the name of dignity, one derives the right to abortion, pornography, prostitution, impropriety or to any other morally dubious practices.

But despite (or possibly because of) these untenable assumptions, the whole concept has become most alluring. What people find irresistible is its simple message: everyone can explain their demands, irrespective of their moral quality, in the language of rights, and once thus formulated these demands acquire both a nobler status and legal protections. A price is paid for this, however. The world of human rights has come to resemble a financial pyramid: what looked brilliant, at first sight, for its apparent simplicity turned out to be erroneous and deceptive. Predictably, aspirations cloaked in the language of rights have grown at a speed that nobody anticipated. New claims, new groups, new identities, and new ways of individual or collective self-assertions inevitably have appeared, and the world is not big enough to accommodate them all. By the same token, the number of potential enemies allegedly determined to take away our freedoms has increased—or rather in the minds of the proponents of this liberal pyramid—and as a result, a spirit of vigilance and suspicion has started to contaminate political life. No system exists that can reconcile these aspirations, rights, and entitlements with the guarantee of new victories over new enemies, just as there is no financial pyramid that can successfully bring its promised returns to an increasing number of investors.

CHAPTER 4

FREEDOM FROM TYRANNY

FREEDOM OF PEOPLES, FREEDOM OF THE INDIVIDUAL

So far, I have been describing negative freedom as a consequence of the-state-of-nature hypothesis and its variations. But there is another approach. We also start with a hypothetical situation, but the opposite one: not that of absolute or maximum freedom but the absence of freedom. The point of departure is that human history began with despotic and authoritarian regimes where freedom was only accessible to small groups who wielded power–chieftains, kings, emperors, tyrants, aristocrats, great landowners, military commanders, and senior ecclesiasts. In subsequent eras, the freedom enjoyed by these ruling minorities was gradually limited and more freedom was accorded (usually under duress) to new groups, either as privileges or rights, or new and more equitable legal provisions. To put it simply, history could be seen as a slow, complex, curved, and yet relentless process of people moving away from slavery and progressing towards freedom.

This view of history is not hypothetical to the extent that we can pinpoint certain landmark events that have made a fundamental contribution to the growth of our liberties and borne a substantial effect on our legal and political systems. Such landmarks have come with the adoption of charters and laws like Magna Carta, the *neminem captivabimus* principle, habeas corpus, and the foundation of institutions such as merchant guilds and local self-governments in the Middle Ages and Early Modernity. They also include mass political movements like the Solidarity trade union, or the Spring of the Peoples in 1990, and the spreading of samizdat publications subverting political censorship in totalitarian countries. There are so many examples that any list drawn up to illustrate these landmark developments would give the impression of a random selection. Of course, numerous attempts were made to reinstate despotism, sometimes successfully, but the seeds of freedom, once planted, sooner or later bore fruit.

Negative freedom in the state of nature was rather disagreeable, being intrinsically bound with loneliness and social anonymity, whereas freedom won in the course of history has inspired and continues to inspire the most sublime emotions. "Liberty! Freedom! Tyranny is dead! Run hence, proclaim, cry it about the streets," an excited Cinna announces to bystanders in Shakespeare's *Julius Caesar* (act 3, scene 1) following the assassination of Caesar, convinced that the assassins had freed the people of Rome from tyranny. In Juliusz Słowacki's *Kordian*, a powerful Romantic tragedy, one of the conspirators planning to assassinate the Tsar promises his companions that: "The half-drained cup shall tumble from the emperor's clasp. [...] And then our country shall be free! Then come the light of day! Poland shall spread her bounds unto the seas, and after tempestuous night respire and live!" (Act 3, scene 4). It would be no exaggeration to say that throughout human history this kind of freedom has evoked supreme elation, given rise to the greatest works of art, aroused nations into action, motivated brilliant minds, driven its admirers to accomplish glorious feats, and encouraged them not to begrudge the most self-denying sacrifice.

Yet, obviously, the battles and wars against despotism were not always fought for negative freedom as such. The ultimate goals were usually higher, more positive, and not necessarily individual–such as a nation's sovereignty or in defense of its identity–but they did not exclude individual freedoms and often openly upheld them. The sweetness of living in freedom, "*la dolcezza del vivere libero*," as Machiavelli wrote, referred as much to the nation as a collective body rather than a system of institutions that protected individual citizens. This view of freedom covered virtually all human ideals and aspirations and, once tyranny was abolished, was thought to open up breathtaking perspectives for society and humanity as a whole. In Zygmunt Krasiński's powerful Polish Romantic drama, *The Un-Divine Comedy (Nie-boska komedia)*, the revolutionary, Pancras, prophesized that "a stronger race will spring, higher than aught the earth has yet produced. They will be free, lords of the globe from frozen pole to pole; a blooming garden will they make of earth, redeem the desert, tame the wilderness. [...] The world will be one vast united home of joyous industry, creative art," (period 4, scene 5).[1]

Contrary to what the negative-freedom theorists say, all of this proves that liberty is rarely perceived as an empty space. People always tend to fill it with their most precious aspirations, usually those that tyranny has subdued, and the more that is placed on freedom, the more the individual and collective experience of liberation is exhilarating. This is, perhaps, the secret of people's natural love for freedom. We attach to it many, often too many, of our hopes and ideals, and we hardly ever distinguish between freedom itself and the hopes and ideals that go with it. None of those landmark events in the history of freedom's fight against tyranny were intended or perceived as solely opening up free space. True, some negative moments–like shaking off tyranny's chains–were there; but liberation was always perceived as heralding positive, higher, and nobler objectives–a better society, a more meaningful life, a better justice system, and more humane and fairer laws.

FREEDOM, REVOLUTION, PROGRESS

But the concept of freedom as a process of moving away from tyranny may easily turn into a dogmatic stereotype, shutting us out from historical experience rather than opening us up to it. The radical version of this view is no different from what we find in the-state-of-nature theory. It can be summarized in two theses. First, everything in the past was either tyrannical, or served tyranny, and therefore deserves to be cleared away. Second, by abolishing prior autocracies we can create the empty space of negative freedom—an institutional vacuum, a clean slate, or a sort of a man-made state of nature—which, finally being free agents, we can fill how we choose. A good example of this belief is that of l'abbé Sieyès who, having witnessed the abolition of the *ancien régime*, thought the revolutionaries would return to a state of nature and expected them to adapt their minds to the new era and behave accordingly. This mood was also reflected in "L'Internationale," the French revolutionary song which later became a Communist anthem: "Let's make a clean slate of the past, enslaved masses, arise, arise! The world's foundation will change; we are nothing, now let's be all." ("*Du passé faisons table rase. Foule esclave, debout, debout. Le monde va changer de base. Nous ne sommes rien, soyons tout.*")

Revolutions occasionally like to raise the slogan of liberty and their leaders have sometimes presented themselves (and have been presented by their lieges and acolytes) as freedom fighters, even if such a qual-ification sounds preposterous. In fact, revolutionary leaders and their supporters despise individual and collective freedom and do not even pretend to disguise the fact. No wonder that those revolutions brought fear, violence, and injustice. To quote Krasinski again from period 4, scene 5 of *The Un-Divine Comedy*: "I saw old dances shining through new shams whirling to strange new tunes, voluptuous dance, the robes were changed, but the old ends were there, the same which they have been for centuries and will forever be while man is man—adultery and theft, murder and license!"

Armed with their ideological blueprints, revolutionaries wanted to create an entirely new order populated by new men. To do that, they had to abolish the tyranny which they believed was represented not by a single person or a well-defined small group of people, but by entire social classes—aristocrats, the bourgeoisie, capitalists, etc. Eliminating tyranny meant eliminating entire social groups, which in turn meant creating a system of terror.

But it was not enough to purge society, often with extreme, sometimes genocidal brutality, and create a clean slate or *table rase* to quote the Communist anthem again. The problem was also the behavior of those social classes in whose name the revolution was launched, which, as if unaware of the gravity of the historical moment and the burden of political responsibility, usually became resistant to the entire enterprise and retained a remarkably strong attachment to the old ways. This required a resolute counteraction; that is, repressive measures and massive indoctrination. "We will use the Soviet rifle butts to beat alienation out of Polish heads,"[2] as one Marxist philosopher once put it with enthusiastic approval.

Revolutions, by their very nature, were anti-freedom and could not have been made any different by more or fewer adjustments. There was nothing noble, redeeming, or naively captivating about revolutionary intentions (which one could appreciate despite condemning their atrocious practices.) Moreover, once we remember that revolution is a magnified, brutal, and extreme application of the-state-of-nature hypothesis, it casts an ominous shadow on the hypothesis itself. One can, of course, think of a much less excessive application of the state-of-nature concept—one more persuasive than coercive. But the whole mechanism remains the same. Some kind of *table rase* is required in order to restructure a society and give it a new modern identity.

A good example of this is an evolutionary approach to freedom. Supporters of this view say that a battle between authority and freedom is not really a battle, rather a never-ending series of skirmishes and adjustments—prudent legislative policy, political compromises and trade-offs, gradual piecemeal accommodations—all aiming to dilute and limit the existing constraints and open up more free space to individuals and groups.

This view looks more sensible than the previous one and undoubtedly is more humane. Yet it is every bit as dogmatic and stereotypical. Both views take it for granted that the past is a carrier of unfreedom and that it should be slowly but implacably neutralized, its instruments of coercion disarmed. In a conflict between the status quo and the future, the status quo is sure to lose; it is only a question of time and the speed of change. The only sound strategy for those with a conservative persuasion defending the status quo would be to adjust the policy of change to the social realities. Defending the status quo for too long, no matter how desperately, makes no sense. The best conservatives can hope for is to minimize the damage which the status quo is bound to suffer as it gradually disappears into an irretrievable past.

This view seems hopelessly simplistic, not to say vulgar, but is worth mentioning if only for the reason that it has taken firm hold in the modern mind. All the revolutionary changes that have shaken Western societies during the last few decades—such as the redefinition of marriage, an all-out assault on language, the politicization of the private realm, including bedrooms, entertainment, and more recently toilets—have been justified by the argument, to use a Nobel Prize in Literature winner's not-so-penetrating phrase, "the times they are a-changing." The changes in question are not just harmless examples of political frivolity. In some respects, they have gone well beyond what totalitarian regimes planned to achieve using the most brutal means possible. The offensive that those regimes launched against privacy, family, language, and thought was partly repelled—at least in some countries, among some groups. In the modern liberal democratic society, however, the defense has been much weaker; in some countries it has been practically nonexistent. It would not be an exaggeration to say that the offensive has been moving forward from victory to victory.

Such offensives are less likely to succeed where societies have managed to create more social and cultural obstacles to them. Such obstacles preventing social engineering are indispensable, and their absence makes a society vulnerable to various types of despotisms. Speaking in a positive sense, one can say that the key to freedom is a richness of deeply rooted social practices that are too diverse to be codified by written laws and formalized procedures, and stem from a combination of social groups and classes, occupational and professional associations, and complex interactions of old and new communities. Whether such a society is more hierarchical and traditional or less so is of secondary importance. All of these historically grounded arrangements produce a complex system of rules that regulate freedom (imperfectly, to be sure) but often more efficiently and more safely than the egalitarian rules of the distribution of freedom which have become accepted in modern states. In short, negative freedom has more to do with Burke's prejudices than with ever new and modernized codifications. It depends on countless contingencies that can exist only in an established, stable society to create this diversity from which people can derive a strong sense of continuity and security.

The evolution of the liberal democratic order has contributed enormously to the liquidation of Burke's and Oakeshott's versions of society. Contrary to the boastful declarations of liberal democrats, extending freedom to certain groups and their claims to public space has not added to an overall augmentation of freedom. Encouraging some groups has implied discouraging other groups: encouraging blacks has meant fighting what was perceived rightly or wrongly as white domination in politics, society, and culture; encouraging homosexuals has meant limiting what has been called "the monopoly" of heterosexuals in all areas of life. Governments could not achieve these ends without creating a system of meticulous legal regulations and a powerful bureaucracy to supervise the new order. Burke's little platoons have been disbanded and political rationalism (Oakeshott's main object of critique) has taken over. The new society has certainly not been Burke's "partnership [...] between those who are the living, those who are the dead, and those who are to be born,"[3] nor has it been Oakeshott's "civil association."[4] It does not listen to "the voice of poetry in the conversation of mankind," because in the new liberal democratic society there is neither conversation, nor poetry.[5]

Some of the changes have been really disturbing because they have annihilated the principles which for decades had been considered nonnegotiable, even sacred. All of a sudden, conscience clauses have begun to evaporate from the legal systems. Doctors, teachers, priests, magistrates, and public servants have had to succumb to new regulations, and no tribunal–either national or international–has spoken in their defense. Freedom of speech has fared no better. Canada's Bill C-16 has made it a criminal offense to use the "words spoken or written or recorded electronically or electro-magnetically or otherwise, and gestures, signs or other visible representation" which may be discriminatory with regard to "gender identity and expression."[6] A recent law in France stipulates a two-year prison sentence and a €30,000 fine for those who try to dissuade women from having an abortion. And France and Canada have not been isolated cases.[7]

FREEDOM, DESPOTISM, AND THE MODERN STATE

The idea that negative freedom has grown through successive conquests of new territories torn from despotism's clutches has certainly captured people's imagination, but it has too many loopholes to be argued in such a simpleminded formulation. Among its weaknesses is an unclear notion as to what constitutes despotism. Typically, despotism is described as the rule of a centralized power that has considerable resources of repression at its disposal, and imposes its decisions on its subjects with mostly unnecessary severity. But from another point of view, the same centralized structure, equally uncompromising in its decisions, has often been commended–at least since the time of Jean Bodin–as the foundation of the modern state. This view reached full maturity in the writings of Hobbes, where, somewhat unexpectedly, the new polity was also inextricably linked to negative freedom, making the relationship between freedom and the state even more complex.

Not surprisingly, in European history the old tyrannies were replaced by new regimes that were hailed by some as embodiments of the new liberating spirit of politics, and condemned by others as equally bad or even worse tyrannies. The 1789 revolution that gave birth to Republican

France continues to be the founding act of today's French Republic, just as the 1917 Bolshevik Revolution is still celebrated in Russia, even though those revolutions gave birth to two systems that exhibited an unusual degree of brutality and were often recalled with horror. Moreover, there are plausible arguments to the effect that what succeeded the old tyrannies were, in some important aspects, their continuations: post-Revolutionary France continued the bureaucratic étatisme of the French monarchy; the Bolshevik Revolution was nothing but the transition from White Tsarism to Red Tsarism.

But even in less drastic versions than those of the Jacobins and the Bolsheviks, the modern state evoked mixed reactions. The emerging bureaucracies might have been less cruel, but still the relentless omnipresence of innumerable anonymous, depersonalized bureaucrats who tied up people's lives with visible and invisible networks of regulations, prohibitions, duties, and punishments, remained. The fear of a new, invisible but formidable tyranny using the latest methods of technology and manipulation haunts the modern mind.

One could, however, argue against an affinity between despotism and the modern state by indicating that the constraints put on freedom in Hobbes's political system and its real-life counterparts, though disagreeable, were nonetheless rational and free from the arbitrariness characteristic of former despotisms. Defenders of Hobbes's theory pointed out that this new, somewhat harsh, political system, though authoritarian, liberated people from stifling traditional social bonds which had been often irrational and utterly irreconcilable with negative freedom.

The modern state was indeed praised as an efficient weapon with which modern man could liberate himself from the past's repressions and prohibitions. Constraints were there, to be sure, but only in so far as they served to abrogate practices and norms that stood in the way of cooperation among individuals and threatened their security. What was not allowed were prohibitions that stemmed from revealed religion, traditions, or from anything that modern man might consider a prejudice

or a superstition. Living in a new state, such as, Prussia under the rule
of Frederick the Great, was believed to be beneficial for mankind. Man
finally found himself in a rational environment which, to quote Kant,
provided "the mind with room for each man to extend itself to its full
capacity,"[8] and was therefore able to leave behind the age of adolescence
in which he had lived for centuries under the tutelage of tradition,
religion, and prejudice.

Egalitarianism was, simultaneously, on the rise in Western Europe.
The sources of inequality were believed to be lodged in the entrenched
privileges of feudal hierarchy and hereditary monarchy. In particular,
the Bourbons' France, with its system of privileges and social castes, was
targeted as the embodiment of historical anachronism. It was therefore
understandable that the struggle for liberation was often indistinguishable
from the struggle for equality; that is, political equality–not equality of all
people created in the image of God. Hence, an attack against institutions
thought to hinder freedom was at the same time an attack on any historical
legacy which the prevailing view of history had condemned to perdition.

The muddle of vantage points from which the state was viewed–as
a mighty enemy of freedom, or as an agency liberating people from tradition and arbitrary rule–created confusion as to what was conducive to
freedom and what hindered it. The French Revolution developed into a
new sinister despotism and a reign of terror, but for many it was a glorious victory of freedom and a turning point in history. Napoleon was
as much a bloodthirsty autocrat as a great benefactor of modernity who
created the institutions and laws of modern society. Peter the Great was
censured for being ruthlessly autocratic but also lauded as Russia's first
great modernizer who gave his country and his people more rationality
and freedom than they had ever had before. Poland's First Republic
consistently resisted the formation of a centralized, bureaucratic state.
It was admired by Rousseau, among others, for its spirit of freedom in
restraining despotism, but also criticized for dragging the Polish people
into anachronism, chaos, and ultimately into a political catastrophe that

lead to their loss of independence. The 1791 Third of May Constitution conjured up contradictory reactions, too. The poet, Adam Mickiewicz, saw it as the product of a Jacobin mind that violated the spirit of freedom, yet was nevertheless the harbinger of a new era of civic liberty.

The same ambivalence has been characteristic of attitudes towards Communism. The Communist system has been denounced as the supreme form of man's enslavement and, at least as frequently, vindicated as the structure whose dynamism destroyed old social forms and made room for new ones. Just as with the French Revolution, the attitude towards Communism has always been ambivalent, giving rise to equivocal opinions: yes, Communism was a cruel and brutal system, but it accomplished a historic task which taken as a whole was beneficial to society. Thanks to Communism, peasants, workers, and broad masses of society got more leeway for the pursuit of their activities than they had enjoyed under earlier systems based on rigidly hierarchical social estates.

We were told to believe that the 20th century was a global clash between two forces—the free world of Western liberal democracy versus Soviet totalitarianism—that had international ramifications. There are many reasons why this stereotype may to a certain extent be true. After all, there were indeed two military blocs; wars were waged; propaganda and ideological campaigns were conducted. Yet on closer scrutiny, the division does not appear to be so straightforward. Many objectives of the Communist system were accepted within the ideology of liberal democracy: for instance, the undermining of the social estates and social classes; secularism; the politicization of the entire society; militant anti-conservatism; feminism and an unsympathetic attitude towards family. This convergence of certain assumptions was probably the reason why there was a patent tendency among liberal democrats, from politicians to intellectuals and artists, to take a soft approach towards Communism.

Furthermore, the adversaries of Communism were not composed solely of liberal democrats. In fact, professed liberal democrats were in the minority because among anti-Communists there were those whom liberal democrats usually disdained—conservatives, nationalists, republicans, monarchists, and followers of various religions with indistinct political affiliations. Ordinary people, tradesmen, administrative staff, teachers, peasant farmers, all with a variety of rather vaguely articulated preferences for a political system, were also against Communism. Many were no doubt sympathetic to the notion of political pluralism within a multi-party system, but their opposition to Communism was moral rather than political.

This shows that the relationship between negative freedom and Communism is more complex than is generally believed, and it is certainly more convoluted than might appear from a simple juxtaposition of Communism with Western liberal democracy. Of course, the want of negative freedom was one of the most noticeable features of the Communist system. People living under Communism could not travel freely, dispose of their property, publish, or speak in public. They were deprived of all fundamental freedoms. But there was something more to it than that. Communism struck at the whole of human existence and virtually all individual aspirations and potential.

Life under Communism was quite peculiar. It put society in a rigid statist and ideological straitjacket, yet at the same time conjured up a sense of permanent instability by abolishing the old forms and institutions. No principle was secure and ultimate, no law firm and unchallengeable, no promise binding. Buttressed by a Marxist-Leninist dialectic, this instability permitted the authorities to dispute and change anything they fancied. What was binding one week might be invalidated the next. In this respect, Communism differed radically from prior authoritarian regimes, which had, after all, respected certain immutable truths. Contrary to widespread belief, Communism held no "one and only" right solution. There was no tyranny of truth, not even of ideological truth; there was no permanent rule about what had been declared ideologically absolute. The meaning of words chopped and changed; the law did not have fixed interpretations and its ideological meaning was adjusted to suit the occasion. If negative freedom assumed the existence of permanent rules and clear-cut criteria, Communism was a system well-nigh completely bereft of any such conditions.

FREEDOM AFTER COMMUNISM

In light of what has been said, one might wonder whether the inspirational joy that arises with the liberation from tyranny, and which artists have tried to capture in music, paintings, and works of literature, is a self-deception? It is always followed by disappointment–not of a psychological but a structural kind–because what comes after the old regime may degenerate into another form of tyranny, sometimes even worse. To be sure, self-deception is not a rare commodity in politics, especially during radical transformations such as the fall of tyrannies. Yet, in such moments, there can be certain types of heightened emotions that accurately reveal the deeper sense of freedom and which cannot be explained away psychologically or sociologically. People's reaction to the periodic crises of Communism and its eventual downfall is a good example of such heightened emotions.

This experience of freedom that the Eastern European countries passed through has yet to be described in-depth or be given full justice. No doubt the negative aspect of freedom was there. One could compare it to having a straitjacket taken off or having a gag removed from one's mouth. A favorite metaphor of Polish poets at the time was "a deep breath of fresh air," a heartwarming sensation which strongly rejuvenated people who had been forced to spend many years in the suffocating atmosphere of a locked room.

But there was something more to it. We should remember that Communism was an artificial construct, conceived as an ideological project and derived from a deeply flawed philosophy that made people live in an artificial reality. That reality was created politically with horrendous social and moral costs. For it to subsist, the new order's architects and engineers enforced absurd rules and induced a type of conduct that people found improper, degrading, and ludicrous. But also, this artificiality was meant to penetrate the inner lives of citizens–their thoughts were directed to aspire to false ideals, their emotions to worship false idols, their language to condemn friends and eulogize enemies, and their moral sense to be paralyzed by self-doubt. No wonder that as soon as freedom was seen to be flickering on the horizon, people's natural yearning was to abolish all those artificial constraints and reduce the tension between the ideological sur-reality surrounding them and the real world that they hoped existed somewhere outside Communism, and which they knew had existed in their own country before Communism arrived.

Remaining on the level of metaphors, one could say that leaving Communism was like going back to a home from which one had been brutally ejected. It was the joy of once more seeing people and objects that one had so longed to see–family and friends, streets and gardens, all the places one remembered and loved. It was like retrieving the unique moral, spiritual, and social environment to which, despite the vicissitudes, one was attached. One also felt that this attachment, though long concealed or subdued by hostile powers, had not only helped one to survive the agonizing years of unfreedom but would continue to be a part of one's life and provide a sense of direction in times of freedom.

Once we understand the existential situation of the people living under Communism, we can see clearly that the basic problem after Communism's collapse was not primarily opening up free space but reconstructing "the old order," bringing back what was real, good, and proper. What had to be done was to restore relations among people who were now freed from an ideological smokescreen, to rebuild communities that had been either dispersed or silenced, to reintroduce and revitalize historical symbols and identities, to reactivate basic concepts and give them true meaning, to revive morality and rehabilitate moral sensibilities, and to patch up the social and political discontinuities.

It was precisely this problem that evoked the biggest disputes in the post-Communist societies. In Poland in the early 1990s, two groups waged a singular ideological war: those who defended the need to create some kind of continuity between what had existed before Communism and what the new Poland should espouse; and those who maintained that the architects of the new Poland should simply shake off the discredited pre-Communist and Communist past and courageously embark on establishing a new order. Being more conservatively inclined, the first group believed that the public realm should contain elements emblematic of Polish and European traditions including classical metaphysics, morality, and Christian religion, as it had done originally. These elements would not be strictly part of the political agenda but form the basic and durable foundational assumptions that political players should respect. They argued that because people had fought for these things under the Communist system, they should be given a proper place in the post-Communist society since they were indispensable to the citizens' well-being, regardless of their political preferences. The latter group wanted the public space to be wiped as close to a clean slate as possible. They often indulged in anti-metaphysical, anti-Christian, and anti-religious diatribes, claiming that the first group's strong metaphysical, moral, and religious ideas had always been used politically to freedom's detriment and that whoever cherished freedom should transfer those ideas to the private realm.

It soon became clear that the conflict was insoluble. Those who demanded that the non-political, foundational assumptions be respected could not help but make them a political issue since these assumptions immediately became an object of political attack, and their defense inevitably obliterated the border between the political and non-political. The other group could not keep the promise to transfer those assumptions to the private realm for the simple reason that they immediately liquidated such space altogether: "the personal is political." This feminist slogan was widely accepted by the modernizers who knew that their ambitious modernization plans faced the greatest obstacles in people's homes, hearts, and thoughts, and it was there that their offensive needed to be directed.

Invoking negative freedom as a criterion was of no help, because the conflict was not about freedom but about a political community's guiding principles. In particular, those who said that respecting foundational assumptions endangered freedom (a basic liberal argument) were themselves quite efficient at imposing new restrictions, some of them annoying and morally dubious. This development (largely unexpected and unnoticed by many to this day) coincided with both the modern world lapsing into new forms of soft despotism at a speed many found most perplexing, and the docility of those who were subject to them.

From the point of view of negative freedom, the best time in Poland's recent history was the short period between the old regime's dismantling and the new system's early planning stages. This was the best of times for negative freedom, not because the country was in a state of anarchy (it was not) but because of the general sense of openness that most people experienced. To use metaphoric language again, we felt many doors opened up for us allowing for many alternatives to be pursued and many scenarios to be tried. As the liberal democratic system solidified, those doors were gradually shut and the number of alternatives and scenarios reduced. Moreover, the number of must-do scenarios rapidly increased, as well as the number of people who anointed themselves guardians of those scenarios, ready to execute the historical inevitability that the age of liberal democracy was allegedly conferring upon us.

The unwillingness to take the new despotism seriously—more conspicuous in Western Europe than in the east—results from the same source that generated a soft attitude to Communism, namely a mistaken view of tyranny. According to this view, tyranny is always associated with structures and ideas deemed as belonging to the past. By the same token, whatever represents the future cannot be tyrannical. It may be called modernization, transformation, education, democratization, liberalization or a dozen other names that indicate a transition from an old to a new political order. The fact that all these processes may curtail our freedom, even if sometimes admitted, is not taken into consideration as a sufficiently strong reason to reevaluate the entire enterprise. The argument that the liberal order may be inimical to freedom is not only treated with disbelief but dismissed entirely as a product of an unstable and perverse mind.

The ideological war that started in Poland in the early 1990s flared up again around 2005, and all the indications are that it will continue for some time to come. In the long run, the way this war develops in Poland and in other Eastern European countries will bring significant consequences for the whole of Europe. This war is still being fought because the conservative side rejects the clean-slate strategy that the modernizers espouse–that is, the strategy to cleanse the Polish minds from most historical and cultural traits and replace them with the current pieties of liberal democratic ideology.

PART TWO

POSITIVE FREEDOM

CHAPTER 5

ON POSITIVE FREEDOM

The second sense of freedom is best understood in contrast to the previous one. If the former was "negative," then we should call this one "positive." The term is well-known, but the meaning varies as the adjective "positive" is attributed to several versions. I shall adopt the meaning closest to the generally accepted one: positive freedom is a set of qualities and conditions needed to achieve important aims.

This sense becomes apparent as soon as we think of all the limitations of negative freedom. Robinson Crusoe was absolutely free from coercion from other people, and yet we could hardly call him the freest man in the world. When we speak of a free person, we mean more than just someone unexposed to external pressure. A castaway on a desert island cannot set himself the types of aims that arise from living in a civilized society and, in this sense, he has far less freedom than his compatriots back home, even though they experience greater pressure from other people and institutions. Crusoe could not seek success in business, pursue a political career, cultivate an aesthetic taste, or do scholarly work. To achieve these, one has to live in a civilized, organized world that provides the necessary resources to do so.

Much of modern philosophy has concentrated on the constitutional aspect of positive freedom, reflecting on the conditions of a system that would offer people not only the space to pursue their activities but also the indispensable instruments with which to fill that space with certain concrete results. Although it would be true to say that both a beggar and a Rockefeller, if left alone, would have exactly the same freedom to sleep rough or spend their vacation in Hawaii, our common sense and rudimentary linguistic intuition would tell us to regard the statement "the beggar is as free an individual as Rockefeller" as more of an unpleasant paradox than as an insight into the nature of freedom. There have been attempts by Hegel, Marx (and the inheritors of his philosophical legacy), as well as John Rawls and scores of authors like him nowadays, to give a theoretical description of the system that offers people conditions which would somehow disarm negative freedom's paradoxes.

But the approach of both Marx and Rawls was not fully consistent with the classical version of positive freedom, which was concerned not so much with the search for a specific political order but with the individual himself. The question posed by the ancients was about the free man's nature; what was he and what were his qualities? The word "free" (*eleutheros*) applied both to his social status as well as his moral and psychological constitution. Despite the diverse quibbles over details, there was no doubt that calling an individual "free" was a positive qualification, i.e. it endowed him with a superior status as well as a set of various personal attributes. Most importantly, the free man possessed skills and aptitudes referred to at the time as "virtues," such as courageousness, a sense of justice, resolution, fortitude, magnanimity, and self-control.

The concept of "the free person" assumed that reality had a hierarchical nature. Negative freedom, it will be recalled, tended to favor egalitarianism because equality seemed the most obvious criterion by which freedom could be distributed–the same scope for a beggar as for a Rockefeller. Positive freedom, however, was invariably discriminatory, setting up a hierarchy in which some people had a superior status while others were lower down the scale; some were more able, others less so; some were more apt to rule than others; some were more virtuous, some less. This did not mean that the very nature of positive freedom implied specific types of constitutional and political arrangements, but it undoubtedly fostered an attitude of cautiousness towards equality as a principle, and towards consistently egalitarian policies.

Let us take a famous section from Aristotle's *Politics* depicting the difference between a free man and a slave. The slave, said Aristotle, was someone destined by nature to be obedient to others; he was incapable either of setting himself any ambitious aims or of selecting the right means to accomplish them. The slave was obedient not so much because he was forced to obey, but because he had an innate necessity that predestined him to obey others. We might imagine someone who was born free but at some time in his life fell into slavery; for example, a prisoner of war. But his status as a slave was forced upon him and should be ascribed to the category of negative freedom rather than positive freedom. Such a person was free by nature but had been deprived of his freedom by accident. On the other hand, if a person who was a natural slave happened to be granted the legal status of a free man, this act of liberation would not change his nature since it was rooted in his innate qualities, not in laws or social conventions. Regardless of his legal situation, the natural slave always performed the duties given him because he could not behave otherwise.

Aristotle gave several arguments to show that one could be a slave by nature. He argued that a chain of subordination was essential to the art of governing so, logically, there had to be individuals who were totally subject to being governed. He put forward three other arguments from the perspective of property, the logic of action, and the rule of reason. Although Aristotle's account of the natural slave must have been inspired by the political system in which he lived—one in which slavery was a well-grounded institution—his arguments were not at all traditional and he never argued that slavery was justified. He did not apologize for the status quo, but rather described the essential features of man's nature as disclosed and made evident within his political context. If one is to be malicious, one could say a vast number of human beings meet Aristotle's criteria for a natural slave.

If this is how we envisage a slave—as one whom nature has preordained to serve other people's aims—we shall have a clearer picture of a free man. On the basis of Aristotle's four arguments encompassing government, action, property, and reason, we can describe a free man as someone who is fit to rule or govern himself and others, with "govern" being used in the broad sense of leadership in politics, economics, family life, and other human interactions. The ability to rule is treated as a special kind of proficiency, one that enables an individual to overcome various exigencies which the world imposes on him and cast off the shackles that encumber most people, thus opening up possibilities for him that the multitudes can neither see nor explore.

But what exactly he rules and which exigencies must be surmounted are far from clear. The free man is looked at with admiration as the fullest achievement of human nature, desired by many but achieved only to a few. But his urge to rule and set his own goals can also draw him into hubris and evil, and finally lead to moral decline. Often, he is described as flagrantly in breach of human and divine laws and headed for self-destruction, which is presented as a moral lesson to those inclined to follow him.

The dream of having the freedom to do good or evil (in either case shaking off the sloth of mere existence to achieve one's own goals, even at the price of defying resistance from other people as well as from nature) is still a vision many embrace today. Costumes and circumstances may have changed and the chances of, and the risks involved in achieving the status of a free man may have varied, but the desire for this kind of freedom has always been with us, and still is enticing even for those whom Aristotle would call natural slaves.

CHAPTER 6

THE PHILOSOPHER

THE FREEDOM OF CONTEMPLATIVE LIFE

For the ancients, there was only one way of life that unreservedly met the condition of a free existence: the contemplative life. A truly free person was a wise man who often (though not always correctly) was referred to as a philosopher, for whom the most important preoccupation was the life of the mind.

Why the philosopher? In the first place, because the contemplative life was believed to be free from our biological and physical needs. If we do what we can to stay alive or survive, if we satisfy our hunger, take due care of our safety, avoid pain, or seek pleasure, our behavior is not free but subject to necessity. We are doing what we are compelled to do by processes we can neither control nor modify to any great extent. In contrast, the contemplative life takes us into a region where no such necessity is in force and where thinking serves no other objective than itself—certainly not survival, profit, or security. From the perspective of the contemplative life, one could therefore look at human existence differently. One could see that all the attachments to worldly matters that have imposed themselves on us from time immemorial and have brought never-ending miseries (despite occasional moments of satisfaction) could be somehow suspended or made less pressing. In other words, one could liberate oneself from untimely concerns, and neutralize the innumerable shocks that flesh is heir to, by developing an attitude of indifference to the transitory character of human life and by bringing tranquility to the rhythm of existence.

But there was more to it. Truth was regarded as independent from human and divine perceptions and decisions. The Greeks discovered something to which we have grown accustomed over the past two thousand years, but for them was an exciting revelation. They found that there was an aspect of life completely beyond the reach of a ruler's will. No one could alter the truth to which reason gave its authoritative endorsement. Truth had such power that even the gods could not change it. Incredibly, the gods instead deferred to everything that reason discovered and endorsed as true. Life in the world of knowledge elevated man to an extraordinary position from which he could look down on the struggles fought by the less fortunate, and even on the gods themselves—at least the Greek gods who tended to be rather complacent about the splendor of truth.

The philosopher's attitude to truth was that of admiration and awe for something not of his own making. He realized an objective order must be respected and that no man should or could, for that matter, circumvent it with impunity. More importantly, he also realized that obeying this order in no way limited his freedom because the truths he discovered in the external world were the very same as those he discovered from internal reasoning. This extraordinary coincidence—that mathematical truths derived solely from the basis of logical reasoning were the same as the truths describing external reality; or that a musical harmony had its counterpart in society and the human soul—always amazed philosophers and inspired them to draw far-reaching, sometimes extravagant conclusions regarding where we as human beings stood in relation to nature and to God.

All these daring claims had at their root a dualistic view of human nature; man comprised two powerful components, the body and the soul, that sometimes cooperated but more often competed with one another. It was the soul, newly discovered by the ancients, that attracted the philosophers' greatest attention and then aroused their greatest hopes. Defined primarily by its high cognitive powers (but also as a basic unit of life and a carrier of identity), it was to change human existence radically. The argument was simple. If the soul was such an important component of human nature then, once it was discovered, it should be given the justice it deserved as a guide to human conduct as well as its driving force.

This was a revolution—one that is unappreciated today because in the intervening twenty-five centuries we have become used to this discovery, even bored and disillusioned with it. It was epitomized in the thought of the great Greek classical philosophers and the possibilities that it revealed for human nature seemed endless. It was as if all of a sudden there was a completely new road open for human beings that would lead them to places of beauty and nobleness; places which, to be sure, were difficult to reach but undoubtedly existed. This sense of a radically new existential situation permeated Plato's writings, particularly those about Socrates.

The soul as described by Socrates, then Plato, seemed to provide a solution to what moralists had long deplored—human weakness. First, there was a clear diagnosis: people fell because they surrendered to the body and forgot about the soul. Then came a solution: people should let the soul control the body. In the Greek intellectual tradition, this meant relying on reason as an instrument to steer us towards all that is good, just, true, and beautiful. Again, it was Socrates who was a pioneer in this respect, telling his friends and enemies that they should examine their lives from the point of view of moral norms. Socrates and other great Greeks were not so naïve as to underestimate the power of passions. But still, they believed it was possible to overcome human weakness with the power of the rational soul.

But the soul could lead us even further, beyond the human condition to defy the ultimate weakness of human existence—death. Since human life was changeable and perishable, and since divinity was defined by immortality and later by eternity, then by uniting intellectually with eternal truths the philosopher could somehow transcend his finite nature and be closer to eternity than any other living person. Reflection on the soul's immortality, such as in Plato's *Phaedo*, would often start with searching for a connection between a rational soul contemplating eternity and that world itself. The true philosopher considered himself to belong, via a well-ordered soul, to another reality. Some expanded on this with an eschatological interpretation of souls being liberated from their body at the moment of death and abiding in the afterworld. Others were content to conclude simply with a soul, well molded through contemplation of the eternal.

Even in times of hardship, philosophy could bring consolation, as Boethius explained in his remarkable work *The Consolation of Philosophy* (*De Consolation Philosphiae*) that he wrote in a prison cell while awaiting the death sentence. When illuminated by philosophy, the mind or the soul could intellectually disarm the terrifying prospect of death by reflecting upon the basic questions of human existence: How far we are subject to fate or chance? What should be the purpose of our lives? What moral obligations does the soul impose on us regardless of the circumstances?

Boethius is a good example because he illustrates the meeting of classical culture and Christianity. Teachings about the human soul were taken over by Medieval Christianity and reinterpreted in the light of Revelation. The original dualism of body and soul was preserved but given a powerful religious dimension. The new concepts—original sin, redemption, atonement, salvation—enriched the way the human soul was perceived. What remained unchanged was that living the life of the soul was possible and commendable, and that whoever lived such a life could overcome some of the human condition's weaknesses, including the fear of death. This life opened individuals to the experience of eternity, though not in the Platonic, intellectual sense. Needless to say, ultimately it pointed the way to the afterlife and communion with God.

One could read in the Epistle to the Galatians that those who lived according to the flesh were descended from Abraham's slave wife, Hagar, and were slaves themselves; those who lived according to the spirit (*kata pneuma*) were descended from Abraham's lawful wife, Sarah—a free woman–and were free, too. Despite the differences between St. Paul and the Athenian philosophers, the word "freedom" had similar meanings for the Greeks as well as the founders of Christianity. People acquired freedom when the soul, not the body, became their master. True, priests and monks lived in discipline and obedience, in conditions that clearly contradicted the idea of negative freedom, but the freedom they had and were proud of was not unlike that described by Greek philosophers and Boethius's philosophy in his final days.

Talking about freedom in a prison cell awaiting death may sound fraudulent, but the charge of fraudulence is mistaken. One should not compare the contemplative life of a philosopher, who in the Akademos garden ponders the idea of good, with that of Boethius in his prison cell and claim that both philosophers' situations were equally free. One should rather compare Boethius's situation with that of a non-philosopher in similarly dire circumstances; then it would become clear that the freedom given by philosophy was not fictitious. In the face of imminent death, the philosopher's soul was neither broken nor paralyzed by despair, but continued its activity unhampered and unintimidated.

Medieval civilization witnessed a spectacular development of communities, institutions, and ways of life that were inspired by the desire to prioritize the soul over the body. Priests in churches, monks and nuns living in religious orders, saints, pilgrims, hermits, as well as laypeople surrounding themselves with religious symbols and rituals–all of this was a visible manifestation that life according to the soul was not only possible but worth pursuing. No one could doubt the soul was a real thing and it had a powerful impact on people's lives, even on the lives of those people who chose the way of the flesh.

The medieval concept of *kata pneuma* was fairly distant from the Greek model of *bios theoretikos*, Aristotle's term for the life of the mind. Rather than living a lonely life, as Plato and Aristotle believed the philosopher should do, medieval monks spent their lives in communities, did not shun manual work (which Greek philosophers thought incompatible with contemplative life), and prayed; the latter activity was not included in the classical version. Yet it was thanks to Christianity that the old idea of the contemplative life survived.

THE PHILOSOPHER AND THE GENTLEMAN

There was one medieval institution that left a distinct imprint on Western culture and civilization and which could be said to have originated from the classical notion of contemplative life–the university. Unmistakably medieval in its form and structure, as well as in its philosophical spirit, the university was a community of scholars who dedicated their lives to theoretical inquiries along the lines indicated by the Greek philosophers. True, the philosophical pursuits were not carried out in solitude, as the Greeks would have had it, but in a community. Still, despite being together, each of them could live the life of the mind. Or to be precise, the life of the free mind, because, as in antiquity, theoretical pursuit was believed to be the free activity of the human soul.

We owe the notion of *artes liberales* (the essence and culmination of university education) to medieval culture, though it can be found much earlier in Seneca. "Why *artes liberales* are so called?" he asked. He answered: "It is because they are studies worthy of a free-born gentleman. But there is only one really liberal study–that which gives a man his liberty. It is the study of wisdom, and that is lofty, brave, and great-souled. All other studies are puny and puerile."[1] The notion was ancient, but its full institutionalization occurred in the Middle Ages.

It came to be accepted that the mind was not attached to any definite practical application and did not serve any useful social or political goals. However, once it had mastered its own cognitive abilities and perfected its tools, it was free to embark upon the pursuit of truth, journeying to the remotest areas of thought and imagination. It was this lack of attachment to any application and specific goals which made the university man a free man. If universities had any purpose, it was to cultivate the free mind.

Let us emphasize once more that universities would not have been possible without a profound acceptance of the body/soul dichotomy, as well as its direct consequence: that the soul's cognitive functions are such an important part of human nature that they deserve particular care and a special system of cultivation (possibly even more so than the body). The *artes liberales* were not intended to inculcate moral virtues but, rather, it was hoped that by becoming aware of its own possibilities, its good and bad qualities, and the nature of knowledge itself, the human mind would be a far better recipient and user of moral qualities.

The university concept had a powerful impact on Western thought that lasted well into the 20th century. We cannot possibly imagine how our world would look without universities thus conceived, but undoubtedly it would be far worse. Universities retained this format for many centuries despite various adjustments that had to be made on account of the specific pressures of time and place, as well as decisions about which disciplines fell under the *artes liberales* category. One has to admit universities did not always perform this function satisfactorily, and sometimes resembled a caricature of the original lofty ideal, but it was generally acknowledged that this was the correct road to take.

In his *Idea of a University*, a collection of lectures published in 1853, Cardinal Newman gave British elites a brilliant exposition of this idea, articulated in prose that used contemporary idioms to illustrate the high qualities of the polished mind vividly (something the book praised). But the book was also read as a defense of the type of university that was, by then, beginning to lose its appeal among those elites. New thinking required that universities provide practical value and serve more concrete, useful objectives, less elusive than Newman's "special illumination and largeness of mind and freedom and self-possession." Proponents of this new opinion were no longer convinced, as was Newman, that "a cultivated intellect [...] is a good in itself [and that it] brings with it a power and a grace to every work and occupation which it undertakes."[2]

Newman referred to someone who had had his intellect cultivated through *artes liberales* as "a gentleman." Was Newman's gentleman a free man in the classical sense? The answer is: yes and no. No, because the *artes liberales* could not deliver what Aristotle promised in his final book of the *Nicomachean Ethics*–a godlike life almost completely independent of earthly needs. The type of free mind cultivated by universities was not the same as the soul, which Greek philosophers made responsible for *bios theoretikos* and its ability to transgress the human condition. Yes, because Newman's concept of the university did intend to strive in this direction. Certainly, university did not liberate a gentleman from earthly entanglements, but it did enable his mind to look at them from a larger, more profound historical and philosophical perspective and thus preclude hasty commitments or rancor. His mind could not be held hostage by the outbursts of popular crazes, ideological crusades, or the premature certainties preached by ephemeral prophets. Nor could it be paralyzed by agnosticism and relativism. His mind did not situate itself in Plato's cold and intellectual realm of philosophers, nor did it feel at home in the philosophical herds animated by burning political passions.

Whether these qualities could equip a gentleman with better insight into and a deeper recognition of the transitory nature of human life, as well as with the inner strength to face fearlessly injustice, suffering, and death, is a question that obviously cannot be answered satisfactorily. Undoubtedly, universities were not meant to prepare students for such hazards, as the Greek contemplative life had intended. Newman's Britain was a fairly stable society; whatever conflicts divided it, it could not be compared to earlier epochs when calamities such as war, violence, and plagues could decimate entire communities, occur at any time, and required (for those who were aware of it) mental fortitude to comprehend the acute frailty of human existence. Although a gentleman's education did not prepare him to follow Boethius's example, he would have appreciated the *consolatio philosophiae* as an outstanding performance of the free mind, not as an incomprehensible act derived from unknown inspiration.

The renunciation of the classical idea of the university, along with everything it promised, started at the beginning of modernity, long before

Newman published his lectures. However, it took some centuries before it spread across Western civilization to win a crushing victory in the second half of the 20th century. This process marked a major shift that dramatically changed the perspective from which man's nature and destiny were perceived. To put it simply, universities in the West severed their centuries-old links with Christianity's and classical culture's founding intellectual traditions. In his book, Newman wrote extensively about religion and its place in university education, being aware of how difficult it was to find such accommodation in his era and how growing secularization could undermine the idea of the university.

Newman was correct. There is a close link between how we perceive human nature and what we expect of a university. Since early modernity, first Europe and then America started drifting away from the Greek/ medieval dualism of body and soul, without which the defense of contemplative life is meaningless. It was not only science and the growing influence of mechanics that undermined the old belief in the soul. The Cartesian soul (*res cogitans*), which contrasted with the body (*res extensa*), did not resemble its ancient equivalent. Neither Socrates, Plato, nor Thomas Aquinas would have recognized the soul that they talked about in the notion of *res cogitans*. Certainly, one could not derive from this notion any idea of contemplative life resembling how the ancients had conceived it.

The emergence of Protestantism did not reverse this problem, only exacerbated it. The Protestant soul–centered on increasingly subjective faith and isolated from a body irreparably infected by original sin–could not embark on any journey towards improvement or excellence either by itself or with the body's help. Aristotle, as an exponent of moral and intellectual virtues, was considered to be as hostile to the spirit of Protestantism as the old medieval Christians who championed sainthood or monastic life. The tension between the soul and the body (from which the ancients and Christians had derived the virtue of self-control), though not denied, became irrelevant since both were deemed contaminated and it was no longer possible to claim absolute superiority of one over the other. Even more irrelevant, absurd, or contemptible was the idea of devoting one's life to religious or philosophical contemplation.

As a result of the Reformation, and later during the Enlightenment, the division of body and soul lost its political legitimacy. Many philosophers, despite innumerable differences in other matters, seemed to share the view that political organization (including education) should be entirely the prerogative of government–preferably an enlightened one–and religion ought to be relegated to the outskirts of social life. Although millions of people, the ruling classes included, believed religion to be true, it could no longer be considered a guiding principle for regulating political policy or education. Wherever it survived, and it did in many places in a quite vibrant form, it was usually by way of historically transmitted and deeply ingrained practices. English and German universities, to give an example, successfully continued this tradition for a long time. On the theoretical level, however, religion was considered anachronistic and harmful.

No wonder that once the classical dichotomy of body and soul had been discarded, philosophers felt an urgent need to change the concept of education. Indeed, modernity was flooded with projects to reform schools, sometimes quite radically. These projects reduced education's intellectual facet and placed increasing emphasis on practice, experience, skills, and usefulness. Schools had to be adapted to a new, modern interpretation of human nature where the soul lost its paramount position, sometimes disappearing altogether, and where reason was dethroned to become, at worst, a slave of passions and at best an instrument to correlate means and ends. In the light of this new philosophy of human nature, there was no place for a contemplative life, except as a form of individual eccentricity to be discouraged rather than admired. Whatever freedom such an eccentric might have (and growing numbers doubted he had any) the contemplative life was not considered worth pursuing.

CHAPTER 7

THE ENTREPRENEUR

THE ENTREPRENEUR WITH A SOUL

After the classical division of body and soul lost its self-evidence as a key to understanding human nature, and the philosopher lost his privileged status, new competitors came along to take his place. Among these, the entrepreneur was a particularly strong candidate. The term arose in the 18th century but did not gain wider attention until much later. The man whom Jean-Baptiste Say and others called an entrepreneur was generally known as a capitalist, mostly under the influence of Marxism which emphasized the new form of property that characterized him—capital. But the Marxist term was not quite accurate: it was not the end (i.e., profit) nor the type of property that accounted for his specificity. What made him an entrepreneur was an activity in which the essential factors were calculation, risk, investment, and innovation. True, he was seeking profit, as most people in every age and society, but profit was the criterion of success, not the ultimate goal.

The entrepreneur has often seemed to many the best exemplification of positive freedom: a person possessing a powerful ability to set important aims and find the means to realize them. It is the entrepreneur who has been credited with building a large part of modern civilization. Without him, there would have been no prosperity, no technological progress, no inventions. Entrepreneurs have financed charities, museums, churches, hospitals, libraries, and universities. Their energy, courage, ingenuity, inventiveness, and resoluteness (all qualities of the free man) have animated modern society and imbued it with the dynamism it has today. Some of the praises bestowed upon entrepreneurs have been prodigious indeed. The entrepreneur perfectly illustrates the religious truth that man is *imago Dei*: his creative power imitates God's creation. "Man the discoverer," wrote the American Catholic philosopher, Michael Novak, "is made in the image of God. To be creative, to cooperate in bringing creation itself to its perfection is the human vocation. [...] The belief that each human being is *imago Dei* was bound to lead, in an evolutionary and experimental way, to the development of an economic system whose first premise is that the principal cause of wealth is human creativity."[1]

Yet when one looks at the classical description of the entrepreneur/capitalist, one encounters a paradox. Certainly, activism was there (how else could the capitalist establish so many profitable enterprises that changed the face of the earth?) but he was characterized also by his profound unfreedom. In his book about the Protestant ethic's impact on the rise of capitalism, Max Weber argued that this unfreedom could, in fact, be at the root of the entrepreneur's extraordinarily active life.

In the Protestant religion, a sinner's salvation did not depend on his good works but on God granting him grace for reasons that must always remain unknown to humanity. Because man's nature was irreparably contaminated by original sin, he had no *liberum arbitrium*; that is, it was not in his power to make a free decision that would bring him closer to salvation. His state was that of *servum arbitrium*, having no possibility of freeing himself from sinful existence and being totally dependent on God's grace, which has nothing to do with man's understanding of justice, mercy, or merit.

What remained for these sinful creatures was pure, disinterested faith with no hope for reward or mercy. There was no way to penetrate God's intentions towards man or anything else. Human reason, aided by faith in the Revelation, (which had previously been considered by Christian believers and philosophers as a good instrument for discerning God's plans and then mending one's ways to be worthy of His grace), was in the light of this new doctrine worthless. God could not be grasped in human categories, and human reason was as corrupted as the rest of human nature.

If we are to believe Weber, this extremely paralyzing mental state inspired Protestants into unprecedented economic activity. While every pious Protestant believed himself to be one of the chosen, there was always a gnawing uncertainty. "In order to attain that self-confidence," wrote Weber, "intense worldly activity is recommended as the most suitable means. It and it alone disperses religious doubts and gives the certainty of grace."[2] But this was activity of a certain type; well-ordered, extending over one's entire life, disciplined, not seeking gratification but performed for the greater glory of God (*ad maiorem Dei gloriam*) "in a systematic self-control which at every moment stands before the inexorable alternative, chosen or damned."[3]

The paradox of the Protestant entrepreneur was that while he considered himself free to deal with "the things that are below," as Luther described them, which he used in most ingenious ways to create wealth, he was also subjected to iron necessities (*servum arbitrium*): the uselessness of good works; work as a calling; dependence on God's grace; and a disciplined ascetic life almost resembling, as Weber said, that of a monk. In fact, it was these necessities that made him an entrepreneur. They also helped establish a capitalist order which Weber saw as a major step towards making a more rational, disenchanted society, one freed from traditional, communal bonds and replaced by impersonal, abstract, legal, and contractual relations, all backed by a strong work ethic.

Not all entrepreneurs were Protestants, and not all Protestants were entrepreneurs. But Weber accurately captured one of the entrepreneur's essential characteristics: a unique combination of freedom and necessity that survived the Protestant phase of capitalism and was present in non-Protestant areas, too. In a way, one could look at the entrepreneur as the reverse side of the philosopher. While the latter lived a contemplative life and concentrated on the soul, the former created wealth by focusing on the "things that are below." But this was only one part of the story. What was remarkable was that, in both cases, the soul functioned as a strict, authoritarian, and disciplinary guardian that kept the body in check. In the case of the philosopher, so that it did not interfere with the activity of the soul; in the case of the entrepreneur, so that it did not divert him from rational economic activity and a sound work ethos.

But as Protestant piety loosened its hold on the soul, the capitalist system gained speed through its own inner dynamic without any regard to religious or philosophical motivations. The soul's role in the overall economic machine diminished until it practically disappeared. How the Protestant religion, which gave the soul such a powerful position in worldly affairs, managed ultimately to push it out of worldly affairs altogether is a separate problem that will not be addressed here. But once the soul disappeared, the entrepreneur was faced only with "the things that are below" because these were the only things that existed for him. Of course, there has always been an individual dimension: many Protestants and Catholics took their religion seriously, even as it related to their economic decisions, but this did not influence how the markets functioned. One could no longer explain the market mentality by referring to grace, salvation, God, *liberum* or *servum arbitrium*, sin or faith.

THE ENTREPRENEUR WITHOUT A SOUL

How did the weakening of the soul's influence affect the entrepreneur's freedom? When his soul ceased to act as a disciplinary guardian, was his freedom increased or diminished? In the final paragraphs of his book, Max Weber noted that "the spirit of religious asceticism has escaped from the cage," and that "the idea of duty in one's calling prowls about in our lives like the ghost of dead religious beliefs." In the new times, when victorious capitalism rested solely "on the mechanical foundation," entrepreneurs abandoned all attempts to justify their activities and "the pursuit of wealth, stripped of its religious and ethical meaning, tends to become associated with purely mundane passions, which often actually give it the character of sport."[4]

Activity devoid of meaningful purpose, associated with mundane passions and having sporting characteristics, has turned out to be spectacularly beneficial in many respects, but it does not necessarily give the entrepreneur the status of a free man in the classical sense. One can even argue that Weber's ascetic Protestant came closer to that status than a businessman in today's consumerist society. The old Christian, Greek, and Roman moralists repeatedly argued that such passions made one much too dependent on them at the expense of nobler activities which required more active involvement. A person was simply carried by their passions instead of being in control of them.

This does not mean that modern capitalism, consumerist or otherwise, has been less demanding or has transformed the entrepreneur into someone whose insatiable greed views profit only as a means of consumption. Far from it. Constant activity, rational choices, risk-taking, competition, innovation–all these have absorbed the entrepreneur to a greater degree today than they did in the past. But once the religious part of the entrepreneur's identity retreated from worldly affairs, questions arose about what would replace it and take on its role, especially in a society which had created a different moral environment.

In a consumerist society, entrepreneurs may be as disciplined and ascetic as their great grandfathers might have been. But, no matter how they themselves behave, today's is a different type of society. For one thing, consumption is now no longer sinful but commendable. Encouraging human appetites, promising people new products and greater satisfactions that lead them into more temptations, has become a rational practice from the point of view of both entrepreneurs and consumers. What is significant in this development is the anthropological change is has brought. Becoming habitually responsive to the external stimuli offered by new products and consumerist pleasures creates a different human character from that which is solely driven by a profoundly internal need to please God through successful entrepreneurship.

This anthropological transition was widely noticed both in European literature and theoretical treatises. The characteristics of a strong man were originally depicted as being self-contained, lonely, sometimes inhumanely ruthless to his neighbors, mercilessly competitive, often insensitive to life's charms, and having a deep sense of individual destiny. He evolved into an equally able market player but one who now was accommodating in his views, sought and provided pleasure, and was receptive to fashionable impulses, prevailing ideas, and public opinion. Originally, an entrepreneur's soul dominated everything he did; later, his soul became completely separated from his entrepreneurship and was sometimes deeply concealed under the many masks he wore. In David Riesman's memorable formula from *The Lonely Crowd,* his sociological analysis written in 1950, it was a change from an "inner-directed" to an "other-directed" personality.

Put differently, one could say that the new entrepreneur had lost his soul, not because he had squandered his chance for salvation but because he had lost his center of moral agency and inner authority to resist outside pressure. Thus, he was composed entirely of entrepreneurial logic and external social and cultural stimuli. This new entrepreneur, despite his vital role in and great contributions to the growth of civilization, had moved even further away from the ancient model of the free man. It was therefore understandable that he did not arouse much sympathy among philosophers, who accurately pointed out that his brilliant handling of instrumental reason in correlating means and ends coexisted with surprising volatility and docility as regards the ends. Left-wing philosophers, particularly from the Frankfurt School, bemoaned his amorphous character, dispossessed of any distinct individuality, contrasting it with capitalism's complex system that provided producers and consumers with superficial, ever-changing collective identities. "The machine has dropped the driver," wrote Max Horkheimer, "and it is racing blindly into space."[5]

If we ignore the socialist language and occasionally pro-Soviet leanings of some of those who turned against the entrepreneur on these
grounds, we discover a sound argument in their criticism. Once the soul
retreated–the soul which told the entrepreneur right from wrong, which
ends were worth striving for and which were not, and how to organize
his life morally–the entrepreneur was swept up by society's current and
had to adapt himself to its moods and necessities. Incomparably efficient
in providing new products, brilliant in stimulating new needs, admirably
inventive in technological development, he hardly ever found enough
strength to contest the prevailing political, ideological, and social moods
or pressures.

There is an argument (with a long history and no concrete author),
that the spirit of entrepreneurship is bound to tear apart authoritarian
political and social structures and, in the long run, bring freedom. This
belief claims the logic of free market capitalism has a subversive effect
because it is a vehicle of modernity that requires the loosening of political
and ideological straightjackets, initially through evasions and semi-legal
practices, then gradually by establishing more or less objective rules. Money,
profit, and economic success eventually must invalidate all anachronistic
authoritarianisms and enlarge the scope of free thought and action. In
short, it is claimed that in today's world entrepreneurs, businessmen, and
traders are, to use Ayn Rand's metaphor, like Atlas carrying the civilization
of freedom on their shoulders.

This seemingly persuasive argument, however, has a limited validity.
It is hard to find an example that supports it; it is much easier to find
examples that disprove it. While it is undoubtedly true that capitalism
gives people certain freedoms that they would not have otherwise, it
does not mean that capitalism's dynamic leads to authoritarianism being
disbanded. Capitalists are unable to achieve this because they are not free
men in the classical sense defined above. They prefer to adapt themselves
to the prevailing conditions rather than strive for something politically and
ideologically risky. Germany's Third Reich retained important elements

of a free economy and private ownership and for that reason it had more
freedom than the Soviet Union, where all forms of the capitalist economy were banned. But German businessmen did not contest National
Socialism's politics or ideology; in fact, they were as loyal and as helpful as
they could be, seizing all the opportunities that that system offered, even
the most inhumane. Had there been businessmen in the Soviet Union, in
all likelihood they would have been exemplary Leninists and Stalinists.

Now that communist ideology has definitely lost its charm and no
longer inspires dictators, quite a few autocratic regimes have turned instead
towards some form of capitalism. And they have done so with a full,
well-grounded awareness that this will not jeopardize how their regimes
function. From Islamic autocracies to post-Communist regimes, dictators
use entrepreneurs to their own advantage with the latter humbly assenting
to the role, not because of their personal cowardice but because they see
a good opportunity. From their point of view, political turmoil is and has
always been less welcome as it often jeopardizes business conditions far
more than stern, but predictable autocratic rule. True, in recent decades,
some autocracies have fallen, for instance in South America and Asia,
and have been replaced by more democratic regimes. But these events
did not happen with the involvement of entrepreneurs, nor because of
the economic results of their efforts, but rather as a result of political and
ideological conflicts. Entrepreneurs accepted these changes as one accepts
a change of weather, either with enthusiasm or misgivings depending on
personal predilections, and tried to adjust to the new conditions.

Perhaps a more telling illustration of the opportunistic (or realistic)
attitude of entrepreneurs is how they behave in the West today. For some
time, the public and private realms in West have become highly ideol-
ogized and politicized, a process labeled with the somewhat flippantly
innocuous and self-ironic term "political correctness," but which in practice
refers to a deep moral and intellectual restructuring of the Western mind.
Universities, media, public language, personal relations, moral concepts,
family and marriage, the history of ideas, literature and art, education, the

courts and legal systems–all these have undergone profound changes, often stimulated and enforced by governments and international institutions. The ever-shrinking number of dissenters have been marginalized and bullied, while "political correctness" has occupied an increasingly wider space in both the left- and right-wing mainstream.

Entrepreneurs, both individually and collectively as corporations, have willingly joined the ranks of the ideological crusaders' army and have spent astronomical sums of money supporting the cause. The notion that money is nonideological, so often disproved in the past, has become completely discredited. All of the world's largest corporations, and countless smaller ones, have launched all sorts of campaigns to endorse what is politically correct, supporting everything from "same-sex marriage" to "gender equality," to use today's standard *newspeak* terms. Many of them have changed the language of their advertisements as well as their internal policies to comply with these standards. None of these moves have been dictated by profit or a desire to satisfy their customers' needs, but by an irresistible urge to conform ideologically. Some of these controversial manifestations could have had an adverse commercial effect, but what mattered more than commercial success was visible proof that these corporations were neither critical or neutral towards the ruling ideological orthodoxy, but rather adherents of it.

The American film industry is perhaps most notorious example of this behavior in today's mass culture. For many decades, Hollywood was ostentatiously conservative. But at a certain moment in America's history, the producers, writers, directors, and actors switched sides to find themselves in the avant-garde of progressive causes. Often, these seemingly profit-oriented people have sacrificed potential profits by ignoring many moviegoers' sensitivities, sometimes subjecting them to unpleasant experiences, solely to impose their own ideological propaganda. The few among them who have refused to conform and have dared to follow a more conservative path have been usually exposed to ostracism and violent attacks. As it turns out, big money in the film industry does not translate into the freedom to make the films one wants but a compulsion to make films that are expected to be made.

If at some point in the future, the West decides to turn away from the dictatorship of political correctness (and let us hope it will) we can safely predict this will not happen with the active participation of businessmen. But once the war is won and the world returns to normal (and let us hope it does) entrepreneurs will duly succumb to the next set of rules and conditions.

CHAPTER 8

THE ARTIST

FREEDOM THROUGH ART

The ancient notion of society being divided between masters and slaves survived, albeit in an altered state more fitting to the context of the modern world. Slavery's new form could be found in the industrial system that was based on the distribution of labor and mass production. Modern civilization, being urban and technological, motivated by the logic of production, and controlled by a new bureaucracy, was said to have reduced the human individual to a cog in the machine, to use the platitudinous metaphor. From Rousseau, to the German Romantics, to Karl Marx; from Thomas Mann, to Witkacy, Charlie Chaplin, and Herbert Marcuse; all lavished compassion on the plight of the modern slave. Perhaps it was the worker entrapped in the production process, endlessly destined to perform the same drudgery foisted upon him and sustained by the merciless profit-seeking machine. Maybe it was the clerk who daily came to his office to perform the same senseless bureaucratic routines. Possibly it was even the capitalist who, though often presented as a ruthless and exploitative modern-day slave owner, was also a victim of the free market's implacable logic of profit which gradually subordinated him to the capitalistic Moloch.

Of the various answers to the question of what might be the way out of this new slavery, one stood out. Liberation was possible through art. Not just any art, of course, but the specific interpretation of art that emerged during the Industrial Age, distinct from the way it had been perceived in antiquity and the Middle Ages. In the classical sense, art was the creation of artifacts according to certain, well-defined rules; in modern times, it more frequently came to stand for the free creativity of the artist's imagination. In the modern era, art and creativity have become what philosophy and the contemplative life were for Plato and Aristotle–an occupation worthy of a free man.

This somewhat unexpected high status of the artist put him not only in opposition to the capitalist machine but often *contra mundum*; that is, against the masses, bureaucrats, businessmen, politicians, and academia. A particular object of his disdain was bourgeois society, not only in its degenerate version but even its exemplary virtues of moderation, frugality, and well-organized family life. To the artist, the bourgeoisie's original and irredeemable sin was precisely its well-organized mediocrity, stability, predictability, and overwhelming sense of confidence that theirs was an infinitely superior society that would last forever.

"Slaves of their own mediocrity." This is the phrase that best captures the perception of those whom artists particularly despised and to whom they perceived themselves in opposition. Let us take two famous works of 20th century literature, Thomas Mann's *The Buddenbrooks* and John Galsworthy's *The Forsyte Saga*, which both depicted the history of several generations of two bourgeois families. Both novels illustrated the clash between the bourgeoisie and the artist through spousal conflict, with the decent, well-meaning, and trustworthy husband representing bourgeois mediocrity, and the wife symbolizing the cold, aloof artist who lacked empathy. Yet, in both novels, it was the latter character who embodied all that was high and desirable, while the former exemplified all that was low and contemptible. *The Buddenbrooks* ends with a young artist who, having been born into a bourgeois family, falls ill and dies not because the illness was incurable because he refused to live in the bourgeois world.

The Forsyte Saga ends with the protagonist, a man of property, dying while rescuing an art gallery from fire. This final sacrifice was portrayed as his moment of redemption, an act through which he liberated himself from the slavery of mediocrity.

One is surprised today by the extreme condescension and scorn with which the bourgeoisie were described (Thomas Mann being somewhat of an exception). German critics, from Goethe to Nietzsche, often referred to the bourgeoisie as *"Philister,"* or as Matthew Arnold put it "philistines." This contempt was bolstered by the notion that the *Philister* were incapable of transcending their limitations to gain even a partial sense of what eluded them. That *The Buddenbrooks* and *The Forsyte Saga* underscored this belief can be seen in how both authors recounted the dynamic between the wife, who represented art, and the husband, who represented the *Philister*. In both novels, the husband was not only less sensitive and more intellectually close-minded, but naturally and irreparably deficient. Despite his sincerest intentions, he was unable to reach into his wife's world and his wife considered his efforts to do so pathetic. Conversely, no matter how hard she tried, there was no way that the wife could ignite within herself a spark of sincere appreciation for her husband's world.

The division of body and soul, so important in understanding the ideas of the contemplative life and of entrepreneurship, had less relevance with respect to the artist. Of course, that the artists had superior souls to those of the philistines was clear to everyone (with the exception of the latter), but beyond this, not much could be said. But the key concept to understanding the artist and his aspirations was the "spirit," a literal translation of *Der Geist*, which the German Romantic philosophers propagated with much success.

What was the spirit? For one thing, it was deemed to be higher than all types of matter and encompassed everything from the psychological and intellectual to the metaphysical and the divine. The best use of *Der Geist* was made by Hegel who, in his philosophical masterpiece *The Phenomenology of Spirit* (*Phänomenologie des Geistes*) constructed his system around the idea that the world had an inner meaning which was not an identifiable, finished concept but an active force which developed and matured through self-correction and enlargement until it reached full self-awareness. The spirit could be objectified in some future form of human organization, one which would accumulate historical and political experiences and harmonize human desires and expectations into a well-functioning organism. But the spirit went further, transcending nature and political organizations, to find its realization in art, philosophy, and religion.

Philosophers who wrote about the spirit spoke of the vertical dimension of human experience, with the highest level being rather obscure and reaching far beyond the intellectual and imaginative capacities of the vast majority of humanity. This level was not associated with any particular notion of beauty, art, philosophy, or religious creed. It went further than anything most of mankind could think of, and certainly went further than anything that could be expressed in words.

Hence the unique role of artists who did not require words (as they did in poetry) to evoke images, feelings, premonitions, and visions. In this, they had a higher status than scientists, philosophers, or priests because they touched the spirit directly through intellectual intuition (*intellektuelle Anschauung*) not through arguments, theorems, or propositions. Of all the arts, music occupied an exceptional place. Being completely nondiscursive and allegedly asemantic, it was hailed as the closest representation of the spirit, comprehensible only to those who were able to grasp its nondiscursive meaning. It is interesting that this view ignored the mathematical constructivist aspect of music that had fascinated the ancients, and instead treated music solely as an immediate experience of the absolute. The problem with Thomas Buddenbrook and Soames Forsyte was not that they lacked a musical ear and remained unmoved by the series of sounds arranged by Beethoven or Chopin that their wives performed. Their lack of ear was illustrative of a much deeper deficiency; an inability to understand music's nondiscursive message.

Art, like philosophy, was claimed to be divine. "There are no things, there are only actions," wrote Henri Bergson. Since the nature of reality is creative there is "a centre from which worlds shoot out like rockets in a fireworks display," he wrote, while God is "unceasing life, action, freedom."[1] What could better embody freedom than man who, thanks to his genius and power of imagination, created new worlds, beings, senses, and ideals, and conceived works that shaped other people's minds and furnished their imagination with images, narratives, and symbols they would have be unable to create for themselves? Artists endowed the fruit their genius not just to individuals, but to entire nations and epochs; the greatest of them, to all of mankind, eternally. "Man, even if born in time," wrote Friedrich Schelling, "is indeed created into the beginning of the creation (the centrum). The act, whereby his life is determined in time, does not itself belong to time but rather to eternity: it also does not temporally precede life but goes through time (unhampered by it) as an act which is eternal by nature. Through this act the life of man reaches to the beginning of creation; hence, through it man is outside the created, being free and eternal beginning itself."[2]

The artist transcended the boundaries of science, common sense, reason, and even religion. He was not bound by the rigors of knowledge and experience to which everyone else was subject, thus he could attain "the supreme truth" and "the absolute" through congenial intuition. The world by itself was bereft of any enduring meaning; the only meaning people could attribute to it and assumed to be an integral part of reality, came from outside–from the artist. Artistic activity was a special kind of *creatio ex nihilo*, an almost perfect imitation of God. Even science and philosophy were believed to be forms of artistic creation. As long as they were not mere pedantic arguments, argued Thomas Carlyle, science and philosophy resembled artistic creativity, having been formulated by the creative genius of individual scientists and philosophers, not by humble obedience to the truth emanating from the world. "At last we have recognized the eternal fact," Carlyle wrote, "that that there is a Godlike in human affairs; that God not only made us and beholds us, but is in us and around us." A man who was an artist spoke to us by means of inspiration, or "the gift of a divinity."[3]

Artistic creativity did not need to be limited to poetry, music, and the *beaux arts*. An artist was someone who, like a poet, created his own unique norms of beauty which subsequent generations adopted as their own and tried to fashion the world around them in accordance with those norms. Or, he was akin to a politician who built efficient, stable institutions, made good laws, inspired others to take action, and endowed his nation with a sense of purpose and identity. Or, he was like a prophet who made people perceive the history of mankind or a particular nation not simply as a random series of events (which is how most people usually perceived it) but as a predestined process leading to some kind of ultimate denouement. Or, the artist resembled a religious visionary who opened people's minds to perspectives reaching beyond their earthly existence, which otherwise would have been closed to them but to which they turned with sincere and profound devotion ready to sacrifice their lives to defend them.

Even if there had been no Newton, Planck, or Einstein, sooner or later their theories would have been put forward, or at any rate theories which disagreed with theirs would have been disproved. Yet our world would be unimaginable without the works of the artists who have shaped it, such as Homer, Moses, Alexander the Great, Shakespeare, Dostoyevsky, or Napoleon.

The world would have been quite different, and so, too, would have been the way we perceived it. These ways would have been fashioned by other artists, just as different artists shaped the perspectives of Australian Aborigines or the peoples of the Amazon. The Polish would have been different if they had had no Mickiewicz, just as the Germans would have been different without Goethe. In none of these cases could these different identities have been reproduced or reconstituted, because they arose from unique contingencies and were not part of objective universal laws like those of physics or biology.

ARTISTS AND POLITICS

Despite his loudly proclaimed superiority, the artist was not as godlike as he believed himself to be. First of all, his relationship with the rest of mankind was far from clear. On the one hand, the artist was utterly contemptuous of the average man, or of people in general. This was the defining feature of those few who not only understood the spirit, but were its executors. Byron's proto-Nietzschean character, Manfred, said of himself that his "spirit walk'd not with the souls of men, Nor look'd upon the earth with human eyes," even though he had "wor[n] the form, [he] had no sympathy with breathing flesh," the humans around him.[4] This attitude soon won followers. Artists deliberately chose to be provocative, condescending, and even offensive towards the philistines, knocking the backwater, narrow-minded folk out of their self-complacency by annoying them and painfully hurting their pieties.

On the other hand, the artist believed that his art was so powerful that it could save people from their miserable predicament and give them some kind of nobility. In his early essay *Art and Revolution* (*Die Kunst und die Revolution*), Richard Wagner expressed his hope that art would play such a salutary role, writing that wretches with "sickly Monkey-souls [...] weary, overburdened day-laborers of Commerce," would "grow to fair strong men, to whom the world belongs as an eternal, inexhaustible source of the highest delights of Art."[5] Juliusz Słowacki, a Polish Romantic poet, sounded almost soteriological when he promised to turn ordinary bread-eaters into angels. So did Matthew Arnold, who wanted to bring "sweetness and light" into society, and Ralph Waldo Emerson who believed that everyone was capable of winning the laurel wreath.

But all claims that artists made about their aloofness towards average people, although sometimes sincere, were dubious in one important respect. The philosopher could credibly make similar claims because he lived a solitary life and did not need to, at least in the most ambitious examples, position himself against anybody. As Aristotle said, his life was self-sufficient. Put differently, the truth discovered by philosophers and scientists needed no recipient. Its reception by society, be it as widespread as possible, did not add anything to its status, nor did it affect the quality of scholarly work or the nature of intellectual inquiry. But art had to have recipients. Even the most elitist type of art inherently looked for specific groups with special sensitivities over others. The freedom of the contemplative life was the freedom of individual consciousness and did not extend beyond it. But the freedom of artistic creation was intended to radiate outward, bringing good or bad consequences for those who were lured or repelled by it. Thus, the artist engaged the world in which he lived with greater vanity and aggression than a philosopher disinterestedly pursuing the truth.

It is therefore not surprising that as the fascination with the spirit subsided and the Romantic concept of the artist exhausted itself, artists could no longer play the old roles of those who looked down on mankind or who intended to bring average people salvation through beauty and spiritual illumination. As art became less about a type of beauty that reflected some ultimate meaning, and instead more self-referential and animated by its own stylistic and formal dynamic, so its interest in penetrating the metaphysical heights (with some exceptions) weakened conspicuously.

Such a development was in a way logical. By concentrating so much on art either as a form in and of itself or as a means of creating forms, artists thought they had reasserted their creative power as well as their freedom and autonomy. No longer obliged, as their predecessors were, to follow convention, reflect upon reality, or strive for truth and beauty, they were deliberately and constantly redefining art, extending its possibilities and proposing new concepts of artistic expression. Art as such became the object of art. Although a majority of artists continued to adhere to a rather traditional view of art as craftsmanship, the prevailing artistic ideology compelled the exemplary artist to go beyond it and transcend whatever limits existed.

The new magic word was "experiment" and the artist became expected to be a great experimenter. Formerly, "experiment" had been a term applied to the scientific practice of reenacting natural processes in a laboratory to either corroborate or disprove the hypotheses interpreting them. Experiments in art did not corroborate or disprove anything. On the contrary, they were intended to create something completely new, exceptional, and never heard of before, which would not be judged in the light of any hitherto acceptable criteria. The word "experiment" is etymologically linked with "experience" (the French have one word for both), but the artistic experiment was the very opposite of any experience. The value of the experiment was the experiment itself. Iconic examples of experiments such as Kasimir Malevich's painting *Black Square*, Marcel Duchamps's urinal *Fountain*, Luis Buñuel's film *Chien Andalou*, and James Joyce's novel *Finnegan's Wake*, were memorable precisely because they contradicted everything that had preceded them and could not be replicated. A black square on a white background was not a landscape or a conversation piece that could be reproduced in a different form but only could be superseded by a new experiment. A white square on a black background, or a red circle on a white one, or any other such variations, could not compete with the original experiment. Equally pointless would have been replacing a urinal with a bidet and presenting it as an artistic statement.

But despite these manifestations of artistic freedom, the artists could not rid themselves of the old problem of being in an organic relationship with their audience. The former contempt for bread-eaters and bourgeois mediocrity not only survived but intensified, as the new art went ostentatiously against the tastes of its consumers as well as the natural expectations of those for whom art was an integral part of their existence. Art's original function of ennobling audiences by connecting them directly with beauty, revealing to them unknown aspects of human experience, or eliciting metaphysical elation, had led to an almost religious worship of art and artists. Now, those functions were ignored as a humiliating kowtowing to all that was vulgar.

Modern artists, as the Spanish philosopher José Ortega y Gasset wrote in his famous essay "The Dehumanization of Art," were no longer interested in reflecting reality. They treated art as a form of play and a work of art as nothing more than a work of art. They utilized irony and self-irony and abandoned transcendental and spiritual meanings. The artists either responded to or rebelled against their predecessors' opinions of art. The dominance of this self-referential concept of art meant not only a higher level of artistic self-consciousness but was to a large degree fueled by opposition to subsequent generations of philistines. Modern artists seemed to be saying: "What we care about is the logic of artistic creativity, not the demands of the majority." However, this boastful declaration was not made entirely in earnest.

Modern art could also be interpreted as a reflection of the zeitgeist. Artists claimed, either explicitly or through interpretation, that they no longer perceived the world in traditional ways and so needed a different, more effective, creative language in which to express contemporary sensitivities and experiences. Malevich's *Black Square* could be interpreted as not only an act of rebellion against the figurative painting of the Old Masters, but also as a symbolic articulation of how a disenchanted world that had forsaken mythology and religious representations of human destiny viewed itself. *Finnegan's Wake* could reflect the fragmentation of contemporary life, while Buñuel's *Chien Andalou* could represent Freud's logic of dreams and associations. Reverting to classical art–to Madonnas, pietas, landscapes, still lifes, and conversation pieces–was as unthinkable as using goose plumes in the age of computers.

One would think that artists' traditional dilemma of guiding mankind in spite of being superior or even indifferent to the masses would have continued into the modern era. But this was not the case. Modern artists still turned their backs on the philistines while attempting to reveal the secrets of contemporary life to them through new aesthetic styles. But there was one crucial difference. Classical artists, in their ambiguous relations with the *demos*, saw their art as describing the world in terms of high and low, with the spirit representing the high and the philistines, with their "sickly Monkey-souls," the low. Having parted with the spirit, modern artists changed that perspective into one of old versus new, with themselves—obviously—representing and creating the new.

This was a radical change. By positioning themselves against the old in favor of the new, modern artists could no longer credibly claim to be indifferent to worldly affairs and thus able to ignore the petty concerns of petty people. In siding with the new, they became profoundly and inextricably involved in the process of constructing it, either directly by ushering it in or indirectly by anticipating it and giving it artistic form. In short, modern art was bound to be political. Concurrent with this artistic trend, political philosophy had also been focused on describing the transition from old to new, or even changing the existing world into its future self (Marxists being the best-known and most influential philosophical tribe to represent that viewpoint). Inevitably, a natural attraction formed between artists on the one hand, and politicians and ideologues on the other.

This natural attraction was sometimes one-sided because often the ideologues and politicians were indifferent to modern art since they had no need for it in their plans. Nor did they particularly need the artists, either. Rather, it was the artists who were more than eager to participate in the march of time headed by political movements. It was not so difficult to explain why artists who made their name by being rebellious, indulged in extravagant artistic experiments, and discarded aesthetic and social limitations, turned into docile apologists for totalitarian regimes and ideologies that severely punished all forms of practical, verbal, and mental disobedience. Once the modern artists had rejected traditional art and felt nothing but contempt for the philistines who continued to cherish it, they could no longer be attached to the world of yesterday or its social structures and political institutions. The flame of aesthetic revolution which they had ignited was easily extended to the political revolution that was to sweep away that already dying world with, as they believed, its anachronistic society and obsolete art.

The Bolsheviks needed neither Malevich, nor his black square. Apparently, it was he that needed the Bolsheviks, for he willingly joined their ranks. The Communists had no sympathy for Surrealists, Cubists, Fauvists, Futurists–why should they? But André Breton, Tristan Tzara, Luis Buñuel, Pablo Picasso and legions of other novelists, poets, playwrights, and composers, not to mention philosophers, scientists, and academics became, for various periods of time, card-carrying Communists, taking part in ideological rallies and legitimizing totalitarian regimes. Those living in Communist countries often paid dearly for this infatuation. Nevertheless, despite horrible experiences either with the Soviet Gulag or its prisons, many continued to be loyal to the Communist party, some until the end of their days, others until the time when being anti-Soviet was no longer anathematized. There were also such artists who not only joined the Communist party but also became active functionaries in the regime's oppressive apparatus. This was the case of the Polish Futurist poet, Bruno Jasienski, who, having escaped to the Soviet Union, rendered all sorts of disgraceful services to the proletariat's fatherland only to find his end in front of a Soviet firing squad.

The sad examples of artists toadying to the political forces of progress did not change this fatal inclination. The old/new paradigm has persisted until today, and nothing indicates that in the foreseeable future artists might find it any less compelling. Marxism's philosophy of history, despite its repulsive simplemindedness, continues to exert its strong influence on the artistic elites' imagination, although nowadays it is no longer treated as literally as it used to be. The class struggle has not by any means been declared outdated, but far greater significance has been attributed to its more modern conceptual siblings, race and gender ("gender" being an invention of the latter-day progressives who have distorted the meaning of the grammatical term and managed to impose it on modern language, thus contaminating it with their ideology).

For several decades now, art has been deeply immersed in politics, and this political commitment has become a part of the artistic orthodoxy of our times. Never since the collapse of the Communist empire has there been such a close union between art and political institutions. Not only do artists readily expound racial and sexual liberation, condemn the discrimination of homosexuals and non-white groups, fight imperialism and patriarchy, unmask new forms of inequality, deride Euro-, logo-, and phallocentrism, but they do so with the massive support of their powerful friends and allies. International and national institutions, world organizations, governments, universities, foundations–all have endorsed this trend, often marginalizing whatever and whoever too openly goes beyond (or even may be suspected of going beyond) the prevailing orthodoxy.

Previously, it was possible to distinguish between the black square on white and its author's access to the Bolshevik regime, pondering on how one could have led to the other and to what extent such a move was avoidable. This duality, however precarious at that time, no longer exists. Nowadays, a shockingly large part of the artistic establishment, including artists, critics, sponsors, institutions, and governments, proudly proclaim the subjugation of art to their political causes. Joining the establishment and pledging allegiance to its orthodoxy has become a far easier way of finding one's place in the world of art today than seeking one's own independent artistic personality. Needless to say, contemporary artists, no matter how despicably servile to politics, never abandoned the old Romantic idea of themselves as free spirits moving along the paths untrodden by the multitude and courageously defying the established truths of humanity's herds.

CHAPTER 9

THE ARISTOCRAT

THE ARISTOCRAT AND THE BODY-LOVER

Ancient cultures bequeathed to us one other model of the free man who, for lack of a better term, we shall call "the aristocrat." The Greeks used the word *aristoi* to denote a virtuous elite who possessed the quality of *kalokagathia*, an ideal form of personal conduct to which the rulers of the *polis* should aspire. Members of this elite were also called "just men" to emphasize their high moral status. This definition did not associate nobility and aristocracy with either noble birth or hereditary privileges. In fact, there were cogent reasons why noble heredity could be considered obstacles to achieving the nobility in question. Aristocrats who inherited their social status claimed these virtues solely on the ground of their birthright, not because they had earned them. The simple fact of being born into a certain family or community did not justify any privileged moral position in society.

True aristocrats have been present in philosophical writings and works of fiction since antiquity, for example, in Aristotle's analyses of the virtues of magnificence (*megaloprepeia*) and magnanimity (*megalopsychia*). They can also be found in texts by the Stoics and later in the 20th century, in the work of writers such as José Ortega y Gasset.

Sometimes the aristocrat appeared as a knight or a warrior, sometimes as a thinker or a politician. He was never associated exclusively with a specific political system or social structure, although he was more at home in some systems than others.

The concept of the noble man was juxtaposed with that of the tyrant and the multitudes (*demos* or *hoi polloi*). One common thread connected the tyrants to the masses; neither group respected boundaries or regulations. Both were whimsical, unpredictable, motivated primarily by desires, and prone to excessive prejudices. If one applied the division of body and soul to them, they exemplified the triumph of the body with its biological needs and powerful, ultimately insatiable appetites. The Greeks used two concepts to describe this tendency to exceed limits and disregard regulations: excess (*pleonexia*) and uncontrollability (*akolasia*).

Both were particularly visible in the tyrant, who sought self-fulfillment by possessing more of everything (*pleonektein*): more wealth; more domination; more gratification; more sexual pleasure. Yielding to *pleonexia* generated *akolasia*, a psychological state in which nothing prevented desires from being satisfied. Some associated such a state with freedom, but Greek philosophers linked it to slavery because it made man submissive to undisciplined, ceaseless appetites that could not be fulfilled. In Plato's *Gorgias*, Socrates called the tyrant's soul "corrupt, senseless, intemperate, unjust, and impious" and compared him to gluttons and drunkards who destroyed their bodies, just as he had ruined his own soul.[1]

For Plato, both the tyrant and the multitudes represented the lowest level of humanity, close to that of animals. In *The Republic of Plato*, he compared the tyrant to a wolf that "tastes human innards" and whose desires were "dangerous, wild, and lawless." The *demos*, though not as excessive or as uncontrollable as the tyrant, was nevertheless also compared to an animal. It was described as "a huge strong beast," one that was potentially dangerous but which could be handled by its guardian, who having learned its moods and appetites could tame its beastly reactions and use them to his own advantage.[2]

The aristocrat was a free man because, unlike an animal, he was capable of mastering himself, resist the moods and appetites that overpowered tyrants and the multitudes, and curb his whims and passions to follow what was right. Just as the tyrant and the *demos* illustrated the triumph of human nature's physical component, the aristocrat epitomized the rule of its highest element. He was distinguished by his wisdom, which was derived from reason's supreme authority, as well as his deeply-ingrained good habits, inculcated virtues, and internalized sense of decorum. From this perspective, he could see how a life subordinated to physical pleasure was not just illusory and unrewarding, but disorganized, vacuous, and ultimately unhappy. The aristocrat's life was different; it was consistent, grounded in good standards, and relatively unperturbed by external circumstances. Even if suffering or injustice befell him, he would never claim that violating rules and regulations would be a preferable existence.

The tyrant and the multitudes could not comprehend how living within the constraints of rules and regulations made a man free, while indulging in *pleonexia* and *akolasia* made one a slave. It seemed doubtful to many people in antiquity, just as it seems doubtful to many today. But these doubts are groundless, and it is easy to see why. Who more deserves to be called a free man: Someone who ignores all limitations to eating and drinking? Or a person who controls his appetite and thirst, eating and drinking as much as is necessary and beneficial? One cannot call the former a free person, because such a person tends to become increasingly dependent on or even addicted to his appetites, losing his power to make free and rational decisions about himself.

The same goes for all other types of strong biological drives and instincts—sexual desire, lust for power and wealth, egotism, fear of death, and a desire for survival at all costs. Once untamed, they gradually gain control of our life and destroy its internal well-balanced construction. A person who succumbed to his body at his soul's expense was called *philosomatos*, "he who loves the body," and it was said that such a person could never organize his own life because the soul was life's controlling force, not the body. Aristotle compared a well-developed human character to an architectural structure that was unified harmoniously by every element having its proper place and function. The *philosomatos* could not create such a structure because his body was unable to function like architecture.

Put differently, being a master of oneself meant that the body should be ruled by what was best in human nature; that is, by the soul and its guardians such as reason, logos, lofty ideals, and moral norms. Just as a person who cared about his body was physically more fit and healthier than the one who fell into gluttony, the aristocrat who cared about his soul was superior to someone who ignored it by being lured into physical transgressions. He was superior because "the health of the soul," an expression used by Plato, gave him resoluteness, resilience, energy, a strong sense of self-awareness, and clarity of vision, all of which made him as independent of external needs as possible.

The aristocrat, therefore, had a noticeable element of lordliness about him. Just as a strong and healthy man looked down on someone who had ruined his body through wild excesses, a man with a healthy soul looked down on those who were paralyzed by their self-inflicted, moral weaknesses and a fundamental misreading of human nature. Socrates had such an attitude. Being the embodiment of the Greek notion of *eleutheros*, a free man, Socrates aligned his life with the truth and moral principles, never succumbing to circumstance, emotional impulses, commonplace opinion, or the whims of the *demos*. There was a distinct sense of lordly grandeur in his demeanor, though he kept it hidden under the guise of being a simpleton. Even his chief critic, Nietzsche, noticed Socrates's lordliness, and occasionally tempered his brutal, rather absurd, attacks against him by presenting Socrates as a strong and authoritative character.

One of the ways in which Socrates's freedom manifested itself was in his haughty distance from things most of his fellow Athenians admired: his country's power, its great leaders, its state religion, and the generally accepted and respected views of its people. No wonder the masses saw him as an arrogant upstart and found his condescension irritating and provocative. Yet despite being a radical critical of Athens's traditions and democratic political order, Socrates accepted the death sentence handed down to him by the Athenian court even though the verdict was an evident miscarriage of justice. He thereby astonished both his friends and his foes, who probably would not have been at all surprised if Socrates had tried to save his life by escaping from prison. But his submission to the Athenian court stemmed from the same source as his distance from Athenian democracy. In both cases, he refused to stoop to what the *philosomatoi* (the vast majority of the human race) would have regarded as a natural reaction to save one's life at all cost. He chose conduct which he thought befitted a virtuous man and was consistent with his life's moral principles, which he did not compromise even when facing death.

The Greek and Christian view that the soul exemplified the best of human nature and therefore should be its guiding force was met with formidable criticism in Friedrich Nietzsche's writings. He claimed that the soul and its lofty ideals were a sham, a sheer fantasy hostile to life. They were artificial contrivances whose aim was to subdue the bodily energy that lay at the root of human action. To paraphrase and simplify the Nietzschean perspective, the real aristocrat was not someone governed by his soul but by a powerful, vital energy. Nietzsche claimed that man's biological exuberance, which in the age of heroic warriors had resulted in extraordinary distinctions and hierarchies, and which subsequently had been swept away by the alleged influence of metaphysics and spirituality, could be revived as a creative force in an aesthetic form. As a result, having been scorned by the ancients and reprimanded by the Christians, the *philosomatos* would bring hope to mankind.

Nietzsche's view was one of the reasons for his immense popularity over the last few decades in Western culture. He inspired the conviction that one could combine two things that classical and Christian philosophy had consistently claimed to be absolutely and irrevocably incompatible: that the body was superior to the soul, thus enabling one's unique individuality to thrive and have the opportunity to make a fascinating journey into one's own world of aesthetic and intellectual imagination. In short, Nietzsche was believed to show how one could have the best of both worlds: being an untamed animal, as well as a refined creator of aesthetic and intellectual values.

The problem with this view was that the primacy of the body brought conformity, not creativity. Nietzsche (who hated the *demos* as much as he hated the metaphysically-minded aristocrats) believed that a Superman, or *Übermensch*, would emerge. This Superman would share the primacy of the body with the *demos*, but without their mediocrity, and the greatness of the aristocrats without their belief in the soul's metaphysical dimension. Such a human being never materialized, even though Nietzsche's faith in him was quite contagious at a certain point in European history. It failed to do so simply because the body did not have the demiurgic potential that could lead to grand ventures, superhuman achievements, or unprecedented self-creation. The growing dominance of the *raison du corps* that we have witnessed over the past few centuries has increased Western culture's demotic qualities to a degree unimaginable in the past. The elimination of classical metaphysics from the modern world's philosophical horizon has only accelerated the process of leveling our minds out to the mean average.

There is no better illustration of this *raison du corps* than the sexual revolution that the Western world underwent in the second half of the last century. Its success was unexpected by many; just as many considered it nothing more than a colorful carnival of rebellious youth. However, it was, in fact, the *philosomatoi's* greatest ever victory. It was a harbinger of the new moral world and a death knell to the old one. From today's perspective, it appears like the last chapter of (or the jubilant coda to) a long narrative about the body's emancipation from the old moral teachings. It imprinted on the modern mind the very same view that classical ethics categorically rejected, namely that the removal of sexual barriers increased our positive freedom and that sexual *pleonaxia* and *akolasia* were a victory over a repressive culture. The triumph of sexuality meant, in fact, the triumph of human nature's basest part. No longer deemed low, sexual liberation became so crucial to human existence that it annihilated all hitherto existing moral hierarchies that had made sexuality subservient to higher goals. There was nothing Nietzschean in this revolution. The actors in this sexual emancipation bore a closer resemblance to Plato's "huge strong beast" that could be easily tamed by clever guardians, than Nietzsche's independent Supermen impelled solely by their own inner dynamic.

Today's body-lovers have managed to dominate the ideological agenda to a degree that would have been unthinkable several decades ago. Their two greatest victories, legal abortion and homosexual rights, have become rallying cries and almost universally acknowledged moral messages the world over. No other moral idea–family, virtues, justice–has mobilized such powerful armies in its defense. There are other body-related issues, such as euthanasia and legal access to certain drugs, that have attracted a lot of support but have yet to acquire the status of a sacred dogma.

As is customary today, they are all covered by the rhetoric of rights and given, as is also customary today, grotesque names such as reproductive and LGBTQ rights. What makes them so powerful, however, is not that they are qualified as rights but that they unreservedly justify self-indulgence. Other rights or liberties, such as freedom of speech (which is intellectual and oriented towards the soul, to use the ancient philosophers' language), have not managed to attain such a strong position, and are easily suppressed whenever they are believed to clash with abortion and sexual privileges. Today, there is no problem in politically and legally silencing certain views so that these practices remain unimpeded.

THE ARISTOCRAT IN A LIBERAL DEMOCRATIC SOCIETY

There should be no dispute over the positive, nay, indispensable role of the aristocrat in a liberal democratic society. Ever since the time of the Founding Fathers of the United States and Alexis de Tocqueville, perceptive analysts of democracy have emphasized the need to reintroduce an aristocratic, or equivalent, element into the (liberal) democratic system. This role is even more necessary today when egalitarianism seems to be triumphant and opposition to its rule meek and limp.

Unfortunately, the sound hypothesis of de Tocqueville and others never caught sufficient attention, and the world moved with increasing speed in a direction that wise men found particularly disquieting. In the eyes of contemporary man, a world in which aristocrats might have some influence looks as fantastic and as grotesque as a world that legitimizes witches, sorcerers, and slave owners.

There are four crucial things that the aristocrat should contribute to the modern world to countervail its ideological tendencies: the rejection of historical inevitability; the defense of the ethics of obligations; an acceptance of body/soul dualism with the soul taking the dominant position; and a classical concept of shame. All of them are interrelated.

Let us start with the modern ideology of inevitability. According to the classical and Christian doctrines, the aristocrat's freedom stemmed from excelling at the rules of a noble life irrespective of widespread social preferences, historical circumstances, and political imperatives, not to mention powerful bodily appetites. The modern view is that man's road to freedom is simpler, marked by clear instructions and signposts. It is enough to follow human urges and overstep the limitations imposed by Christian religion and classical philosophy. *Akolasia* and *pleonexia* are no longer viewed as sins or transgressions to be avoided or feel guilty about when committed; they are vehicles of emancipation.

Today's road to freedom, although envisioned as going forward, looks like a return to nature—the shrugging off of all the unnecessary artifices that were created out of ignorance, fear, and irrational sentiments. This change has been declared largely as a one-way process, a transition from artificial inconvenience to natural convenience where, having reached the destination, going back to the old state of affairs seems unimaginable. Or, to use a different image, as unburdening oneself from cumbersome and excessive objects long believed to be intrinsic. Put in more philosophical terms, it has been a gradual victory for the body which, as everyone knows, very much exists and demands to have its needs fulfilled, over the soul, which may or may not exist, but whose claims have come to be perceived as irritatingly unrealistic.

All this has given the process of the body's emancipation a trait of inevitability. It is generally perceived that there was something relentless in the body's victory over the soul. This inevitability resembled an unstoppable, predetermined process, akin to moving from fiction to reality, from alchemy to chemistry, from witchcraft to medicine, from Byzantine etiquette to simple rules of conduct, from royalism to democracy. This process is believed to illustrate the natural course of human development, which meant that the body's triumph had to come about sooner or later and that any attempt to hinder its offensive was doomed to fail.

It can be counterargued, however, that positive freedom makes little sense if it amounts to adapting oneself to changing conditions and to one's biological inclinations. Socrates would not have deserved to be called a free man if he had followed the advice of the *philosomatoi*, which was undoubtedly consonant with every person's attachment to life, and escaped from prison. He would have prolonged his life, to be sure, and rescued his negative freedom, but he would have betrayed the standards that he himself accepted and regarded as inviolable. He no longer would have been his own master, but would have capitulated to everything he considered alien. Not to mention, his reputation and moral stature as an aristocrat would have suffered enormously. Giving up one's own principles out of the fear of death was a shameful act, unworthy of a free man.

As regards the modern liberal democrat who represents the class of victors in this process of emancipation, despite his loud bragging about transgressions, too much of his language and presuppositions sound discordant with the idea of freedom—too much necessity, inevitability, irreversible change, and too many natural God-given drives. His language holds too many references to the tides of history and refers to excessive adapting, yielding, giving in, and indulging. There is also too much easiness in pursuing freedom, too much self-absolution, and too much nonchalance in dismissing all the caveats and counterarguments accumulated over the centuries. He appears more like an actor who takes part in a performance in which he has been ordered to play the role of a free man. He duly obeys the author's and the director's orders but is utterly unaware that, by listening to those orders, he has already lost his chance to be his own master.

The aristocrat in a liberal democratic society reenacts this ancient drama with Socrates and others as its protagonists. The aristocrat is one of the final defenders of the soul in its classical understanding (with the loftier portion controlling the lower portion). It would be historically correct say that the soul he defends predates the body-lovers' revolution of 1968 and its earlier chapters, but this is the perspective that the aristocrat would not accept. The true aristocrat makes it clear that any decision about his soul cannot be measured in pre- or post-revolutionary terms, by democracy or pre-democracy, liberalism or illiberalism, or by such notions as anachronism, progress, the dustbin of history, or historical inevitability. Whoever defines himself by such criteria (and today it is common practice) deserves to be called a slave in Aristotle's sense, rather than a free man.

The aristocrat embraces this philosophy of human nature not only because his refined taste reinforces the distinction between high and low, but primarily because he believes that the principles and qualities which make a free man are essentially immune from historical contingencies. In this, the aristocrat differs from the modern man. What makes the latter a willful victim and, at the same time, a devout worshipper of historical necessity is a notion that over the past few decades has become the fundamental creed of our times: we, as human beings, are primarily and exclusively rights-bearing people and, as such, are beneficiaries of progress. Anyone who believes in rights is prone to see the history of civilization as the slow process of more people gaining ever more rights. This criterion is so commanding that whoever adheres to it cannot but feel a deep aversion towards previous epochs and societies which had not been blessed with those rights. This is specific to our times. Believing in the unconquerable power of history, we despise history and perceive the past only as a record of horrendous deviations from the pieties that today's ideology sanctifies. In this, the liberal does not differ much from the Marxist.

The aristocrat is defined by his obligations, not by his rights. Those obligations do not easily evolve over time and remain relatively untouched by historical change. Patriotism, with its wide spectrum of actions and emotions, means roughly the same to patriots today as it did in previous centuries. Any changes are accidental, but they don't change the essence. During a period of prolonged peace, dying for one's country may not be something that preoccupies people's minds and is usually thought of as absurd, but it still constitutes a living part of patriotism's tradition. Yet it is extraordinary how in times of ultimate necessity people living in peaceful, even somewhat decadent, societies find the inner strength to sacrifice their lives for their country and suddenly understand the wisdom of the old Roman maxim, "it is sweet and fitting to die for the homeland" (*dulce e decorum pro patria mori*).

The same can be said about other important obligations such as to one's family, to God, to one's honor, friends, and vocations. Historical and civilizational transformations might alter how they appear and are articulated, but they remain the same obligations. One can imagine different ways of betraying one's friends, depending on the historical epoch in which one lives, but having an obligation to a friend remains unchanged. All of those obligations are fairly stable in contrast to the rights which have evolved with increasing speed. What count as rights today would not have been called rights two decades ago. One shudders at the thought of what new rights might appear in a not too distant future.

In accepting obligations today, as well as in the past, one sees in them the primary moral dimension of one's life and thus assumes the body/soul dualism. How the soul is understood—be it religiously, metaphysically, as a vague intuition, part of cultural tradition, or even symbolically—does not matter so long as it is understood to be sovereign vis-à-vis the body and independent from the power of historical fluidity. Allowing oneself to be governed by the body and succumb to what seems historical necessity is considered a slavish attitude. Controlling the body and resisting history's ever-changing moods is the mark of a free man.

A rights-bearing person, on the other hand, is not attached to the body/soul dualism. In fact, he does not need it and is increasingly reluctant to accept it. While it is true that, in the past, this dualism was invoked as a possible rationale for the concept of natural rights–the body did not seem dignified enough to claim rights by nature–subsequent developments have made the soul increasingly redundant. The whole point of rights is that they induce us to get rid of as many obstacles as possible which might stand in the way of our claims and entitlements. The soul, which might slow down or even block these obstacles' removal, is therefore unnecessary and may be dispensed with as a potentially oppressive instrument.

One can see how the Catholic Church (a typical aristocratic institution) has evolved in recent years, drifting in the opposite direction as a result of espousing the doctrine of rights. Having accepted that doctrine, the Church has become infected with the logic of the growing dominance and number of rights. Predictably, some cardinals, bishops, and rank-and-file priests have accommodated themselves gradually to new moral opinions, for instance concerning homosexuality, to which the Church had been categorically opposed for centuries. Once they incorporated the language of rights into their own discourse, they found themselves taking a defensive position against all those who demanded new privileges for themselves and articulated their demands using this language. There is no way, while staying within this doctrine, that one can restrict rights only to those who at a certain historical moment were thought compatible with Catholic teaching. Rights grow in number and in scope, and each time new ones appear they are heralded with the same unflinching dogmatism as all previous declarations. Whoever embraces the doctrine will sooner or later yield.

The aristocrat is also the guardian of our sense of original shame, which was grounded in the hierarchic view of the soul. Shame was the reaction of human nature's loftier elements to the incursions of its baser instincts. We felt ashamed when we did or said something that contradicted these high standards, and when we knew that by doing or saying something we were giving in to temptations, weaknesses, or morally dubious desires. Whoever treated those standards seriously felt shame for falling below them. This traditional view of shame has been changing for some time, mostly due to the growing influence of "the love of the body" (*somatophilia*). Now it is nature's basest standards that make the higher standards ashamed. To express it somewhat metaphorically, it is the body that puts the soul to shame. Once the vehicles of the soul—religion, metaphysics, and the ethics of virtue—had been deprived of their function, mostly because they were deemed outdated, it became embarrassing to refer to their authority.

Since vulgarity has been considered an element of historical inevitability, it has become more shameful to oppose it than to condone it or even engage in it. Since pornography is now believed to be a necessary aspect of modern life, criticizing it as a danger to one's soul causes embarrassment rather than garners support. Since the omnipresence of sexualization is perceived as an achievement of our times, being against it is more shameful than transgressing whatever sexual taboos remain.

These are then the four interconnected areas in which the aristocrat can make a difference both in theory and in practice. But his is not an easy task. The ideology of inevitability appears invincible because it survives on egalitarianism, which has been on an apparently victorious march for several centuries. The ethics of obligations has a formidable enemy in the ethics of rights, which is generally acclaimed to be the first and the only truly universal religion in mankind's history. The classical concept of the soul is difficult to defend in a deeply secularized environment. And without the soul, the classical mechanism of shame cannot be restored.

The obstacles are powerful and one should not be surprised that the high aspirations that the aristocrat sets for himself clash with what the rest of mankind finds obvious and appealing. In historic aristocratic societies (at least ones that hypothetically were more inclined to assimilate his ideas) the aristocrat's life was not easy. His failure to convince the ruling elites ultimately failed to curb the excesses of impending egalitarianism. In a liberal democratic society, he represents that which is unusual and wanting. Whether this is an asset or a liability remains to be seen.

PART THREE

INNER FREEDOM

CHAPTER 10

ON INNER FREEDOM

The third sense of freedom concerns authorship of one's actions, words, and thoughts. I am free insofar as I, and I alone, am the author of what I do, say, and think. If what I do, say, and think has been imposed upon me, if other people's sly persuasion or manipulation has induced me to do those things, or if I have imitated others thoughtlessly, I no longer exercise my freedom because it is not the real me behind all those decisions.

In the concept of positive freedom, one references external criteria to fashion for oneself a suitably free existence. In the concept of inner freedom, objective criteria do not count. My goal is to adapt my actions, words, and thoughts not to the model of the entrepreneur, artist, or aristocrat but to what I consider, and have a good reason to identify as, the real me.

This notion can be easily grasped in the case of people who, having committed something morally reprehensible, later try to prove their innocence by claiming they were unable to control their actions. It is a standard line of defense for those who face the gravest criminal charges. They say that at the moment they committed the crime, they were in a state of wild passion and could not contain themselves. It is also a standard line of defense for those who were responsible for political horrors, either directly as perpetrators or indirectly as administrators or apologists for the reign of terror. Some of the accused say they were coerced into doing evil things. Others argue that their minds were paralyzed by criminal propaganda which, like a hypnotic drug, made their character supple in the hands of their superiors. "I was not myself." "My mind was shackled by ideology." "I renounced my own individual will and subjected myself to the will of the Party." "I was coaxed by propaganda." All are the typical phrases renouncing personal responsibility.

Czesław Miłosz's *The Captive Mind* describes how certain Polish writers became mentally captivated under Communism and adopted a set of ideas which they found so compelling that they surrendered themselves to the most inhumane system ever contrived in human history. Whether deep down in their hearts and in their true selves they were different, we cannot know for sure. Some of them apparently were different, considering that later on they denounced their own erstwhile Communist involvement. But Miłosz (who himself was not entirely blameless in this respect) was correct that the captive mind existed, and that it either willingly or unwillingly became possessed by an idea or ideological passion, or simply relinquished any autonomous aspirations.

The protagonists of Miłosz's book, who lived long enough to feel ashamed of what they had said and done in the past, clearly believed that their characters had been altered. Verifying their confessions would be difficult indeed, but the fact that they treated their own fall as a form of intoxication or asphyxiation shows that they thought themselves to have been the victims of enslavement rather than the enslavers. Put differently, the fact that they enslaved others resulted from the anterior subjection of their minds to Communism's sinister ideology.

This type of freedom—for convenience let us call it inner freedom—coincides to a large extent with what we call authenticity. Matthew Arnold wrote that there was a powerful and mysterious undercurrent of authentic experience that flowed below what we did in our ordinary life. Thus, inner freedom meant not only that the various layers of our experience were in harmony with each other, but also that this undercurrent of our true experience determined how we lived and what we stood for. This core of our individuality should, like a stream, penetrate our entire life from small things to major decisions, from aesthetic taste to basic moral judgements, outweigh external criteria, and sometimes even defy existing rules.

Imagine a person living in a world that offers him a broad range of well-protected personal liberties, who has achieved much in his professional career and social life, who is not prevented from speaking his mind or having his own opinions, but who at a certain moment in his life realizes that everything that he has done, said, and believed up to that point was not his own. He gives up his career, discards the attitudes which he had once accepted but which now he sees as incompatible with his true self, and decides to do something completely different. It might even be a decision which will put certain limits on his positive and negative freedoms. He might, for instance, isolate himself from society, live on a farm, or enter a monastery. But he will claim that from that moment on he will have an overpowering sense of being a free person because everything he subsequently does and says will be only his.

This concept of freedom immediately gives rise to a problem: whether one is or is not oneself seems to be an entirely subjective opinion that cannot be verified externally. If I swear that what I do and stand for is my very own, it is extremely problematic for any outside authority to challenge that conviction. We have had examples of people who willingly identified themselves, body and soul, with movements that any elementary intelligence would qualify as silly and irrational; and other people who sacrificed their lives for what outside observers rightly considered absurd. In either instance, it would have been futile to have tried to prove their gullibility to them and dissuade them from their beliefs. The writers in Miłosz's book clearly believed that, while they were enchanted with Communism, their identification with the regime was impeccably genuine. There were no grounds for doubting their sincerity. So, one can ask, when were they authentic? Before when they were Communist apparatchiks? Afterwards, when they became anti-Communist dissidents? In both roles? Or perhaps, some might say, in neither, because on both occasions, whether being Communist or anti-Communist, they were floating with the current.

In spite of these ambiguities, we generally believe in the value of being authentic. In defiance of authenticity's profound subjectivity, most of us claim to have little difficulty in distinguishing between those whose words and conduct are natural and sincere, and those whose words and conduct are constructed from the scraps of other people's views and actions. The discord between someone's inner core of existence and their outer appearance always reveals itself, no matter how much the person might try to assimilate the two. We can immediately recognize the falsehood and can clearly see that such people are not what they pretend to be.

This seemingly contradictory aspect of inner freedom is easy to understand, particularly in modern societies which, over the past few centuries, have been agitated by outbursts of often totalitarian mass movements, and exposed to increasingly efficient ways of organizing people's minds and shaping their innermost preferences. This has generated two clearly opposed yet mutually reinforcing tendencies. On the one hand, there has been a growing awareness that one needs to be different from others and to have an unquestionably unique identity; on the other, there has been an equally strong desire to join groups and to assimilate oneself with collective identities. One is presented with two unfolding contradictory spectacles when one watches people commit themselves to mass movements, fashions, ideologies, those who sell and who buy, or those who elect and are elected. On the one hand, we witness the desperate attempts of individuals to manifest the exceptional nature of their true selves through the sincerity of their words and actions; and, on the other hand, we witness a most depressing parade of captive minds, chanting the same clichés in unison and mimicking whatever they have been told to mimic.

These two developments seem to bolster one another. As the process of homogenization has accelerated, individuals have become increasingly less distinguishable in their views, conduct, language, and actions, thus rendering the search for one's uniqueness all the more urgent. Individuals have had to bury their uniqueness ever deeper within their nature in the hope that the new wave of collectivism would not touch it. But this wave has continued its onslaught and what was once believed to be the most intimate carrier of one's individuality has quickly surrendered to it. Sex is probably the best illustration of this. Even though it concerns an individual's particular personal experience, sex has in recent decades transformed into a powerful instrument for creating collective ideologies that regulate life's most private aspect.

Feminism is another good illustration of this tendency. The concept began with the assumption that women's identity had been hijacked and enslaved by the centuries of men's perfidious oppression and that women should finally be free to express their feminine concerns and interests, and articulate them in a feminine language that was part of a larger all-encompassing feminine world view. But this initially libertarian plan instantaneously transformed itself into a rigid orthodoxy, imposing miniscule rules and regulations not only on women, but on society as a whole. It codified the rules of language, rewrote history, and forced others to succumb to new, politically correct versions. It condemned ideologically suspect thoughts, gestures, and emotions, and made laws increasingly inquisitorial. Since Marxism's demise, there has been no other ideological movement in recent history that has managed to produce as many captive minds as feminism.

The question of the extent of inner freedom will depend on a more basic question: what is "my own self"? If I am to be free insofar as my decisions are my own, then which part of me makes those decisions? Is it reason, or my will, or perhaps the cravings of my soul? Do we speak of a primitive "self" prior to all education, the "self" of a child or a savage? Or, when we say "my own self," do we mean only "my mature and developed personality"? There is a dearth of possible definitions of "my own self," and each of them gives a different picture of inner freedom. If "I, myself" consists only of my reason, then any submission to passion and desire will be considered a state of enslavement. But if "my own self" includes my cravings too, then a manifestation of my inner freedom will be the satisfaction of my own desires. Am I free when I eschew the temptation of leisure and devote myself to my work and duties, or, am I cast into subjugation when I turn down entertainment? Which type of education enhances "my own self," and which might deprive me of my own authenticity?

CHAPTER 11

THE NONEXISTENT SELF

BETWEEN SKEPTICISM AND CONSERVATISM

Let us start by considering the simplest hypothesis: there is no "self," therefore, there is no pre-existing unifying thread that effectively integrates our actions and thoughts. In such a view, a person's identity is a random collection of various elements, a mixture of innate qualities and external influences accumulated and structured over the course of one's life. Some have compared a person's identity to a wax tablet on which each of his successive experiences leaves its own imprint. Others have likened it to a theatre stage on which we act out plays written by others, trying to contribute (successfully or otherwise) individual traits of interpretation. Others have said self-identity resembles a play in which each of us tries to write our own lives, putting all of the successive components together into various narratives that might not be always consistent with one another.

An example of this hypothesis can be found in the language of Homer where, as Bruno Snell indicated some decades ago, there were no words for "body," "soul," or "mind" as such, but instead several words that indicated various aspects of what later would be identified as the body and the soul. Snell argued (though not everyone agreed) that Homer's Greeks did not perceive themselves as unified human beings and that their basic existential experience was fragmented. Their bonds were not internal but external, influenced by tradition, custom, and socially transmitted practices. To use modern jargon, what unified Homer's characters was their unwitting acceptance of, and conformity to, their social roles.

This explains the duality which every careful reader of Homer's masterpieces cannot fail to notice. The Homeric man exudes strength and courage, even recklessness and arrogance, sometimes brutality and cruelty, and a hubristic disregard for existing norms. In short, he feels free to do anything he wants. Yet Homer's heroes and heroines have a latent respect for the roles they are supposed to play, as well as a sense of being a part of a larger plan (not of their own making) that will finally decide their destiny. Even the unruly and somewhat mentally sluggish Achilles succumbed to this belief.

Thus, the Homeric man's fragmentation had two sides: one superficial; the other, more profound. Superficially, the fragmented man seemed to know no inhibitions in manifesting his dispersed, contradictory, and disorganized inclinations. That said, his actions were informed by both a powerful, though unclear set of external rules, as well as an unidentified, unfathomable compulsion that was stronger than the will of men and gods, from which there was no recourse and which carried no reassuring message.

Classical philosophy and later Christian thought challenged this view and made the strongest philosophical argument ever that the human self does exist and that it has a powerful metaphysical core. Modernity, however, rejected Christian medieval philosophy and approached classical Greek philosophy rather selectively–taking the secondary ideas while ignoring the essential ones–to resurrect the notion of the fragmented human self, this time in a far less dramatic cultural context than that of Homer's heroic world.

It is to David Hume that we owe the most influential argument which deprived the self not only of its metaphysical core but also of its unity. "I may venture to affirm of the rest of mankind," wrote Hume, "that they are nothing but a bundle or collection of different perceptions, which succeed each other with an inconceivable rapidity, and are in a perpetual flux and movement."[1] Hume drew this conclusion by dissecting human consciousness and reducing it to its basic constituents. What he found at the end of this dissection was not a unified substance of the self, but a cluster of independent elements which we, in the course of our life, try to integrate as much as we can, but which remain what they were to begin with; that is, a cluster of independent elements.

The surprising thing about Hume was that this rather disturbing view of human nature did not push him to any comparably disturbing conclusion. He resorted to the device of *mutatis mutandis* which we found in Homer; that is, to the influence of external forces, mainly social rules. We were, Hume claimed, stabilized from outside, and what gave our existence a sense of unity were habits, social practices, and a general rootedness in society. In the process of its evolution, society developed certain rules of cooperation, for instance through commerce and a system of property, that bound people together and built a network of meanings and references around each of them. Once people had those, the philosophical unity of the individual self, or lack thereof, became irrelevant. Custom, that "great guide of human life,"[2] as Hume put it, endowed our amorphous identity with a provisional though effectively enduring continuity.

It is something of a paradox that Hume coupled the nonexistence of the unified self with a social conservatism built on the power of custom. One might call this conservatism skeptical or, as Hume's critics said, "cynical," but it was conservative nonetheless because it assumed that human nature could be tamed by social conventions which contained wisdom far older than any individual. No wonder that Hume rejected contractarianism as well as the state-of-nature theory on which it was based, both of which placed humans above social conventions.

We cannot really answer the question of how free Hume's man was (i.e., to what extent he was himself), because this theory asks the wrong question. He could not live without social conventions; in fact, he did not exist without those conventions. Therefore, he did not perceive conforming to them as being detrimental to his authenticity. What we could say of him is that he was characterized by a moderate, gentle, even decent skepticism and complied with custom but, at the same time, distrusted overly aggressive collective identities and overbearing attempts to fence in human existence within a fixed set of strictures. His lenience to the inertia of custom went hand in hand with his hostility towards attempts to foist upon him an unequivocal understanding of what was meant by "the human self," such as those found in classical philosophy or mainstream Christianity.

Even if, or perhaps *because* custom cannot be fully justified and rationalized, it would still be a better way of living for an individual and his sense of inner freedom than the philosophical profundities of classical philosophy, which the skeptical Hume found rather harmful and an unbearably restrictive façade. In short, Hume's society would be inhabited by civilized, well-organized, prudent, and cooperative people, drawn to common sense and therefore distrustful of great metaphysical adventures. Predictably, they would only direct their ire against those who pushed humanity towards such adventures. Such a society would not be prey to the anxiety that we found in Homer's, with its awareness of destiny, troubling uncertainty, and fear of the unknown.

But is this combination of cynical, social conservatism, and cognitive skepticism viable? How resistant would people's conservative habits be towards the gnawing awareness that all that they think and do is provisional? One possible answer would be that this conservatism could exist only as long as there were enough people who believed in its beneficial consequences. Once that belief was gone, conservatism would disappear for good.

Hume did not entertain such a scenario, but Blaise Pascal did. Pascal, too, had serious doubts about whether it was possible to determine the "human self," and perhaps even whether it existed at all, though for reasons quite different from Hume's. "Where, then, is this Ego," he asked, "if it be neither in the body nor in the soul?"[3] His doubts lead him to hope (with what we would now call a naïve outlook predating Hume) that people still believed in the world's moral and spiritual orderliness. Pascal's advice was: let the wise (*les savants*) speak up in defense of simple folk and appreciate their role in the world since they were the ones who sustained society's beneficial conventions.

There was another group which Hume never mentioned, but which Pascal feared: *les demi-savants*.[4] These "half-learned ones," or wiseacres, were motivated by their intellect's destructive power to decimate the simplicity and naivety of simple folk's beliefs. No one who passed through their skepticism and demystification programs could sincerely hold the view that "custom is the great guide in human life." Custom could survive only in integrated selves. They made the power of custom possible through repetition, predictability, and clearly defined social roles. To imagine that custom could keep fragmentary selves in relative stability was to reverse the cause-effect relationship. Custom could be only the effect of such selves, not its cause.

Was Hume *un demi-savant*? Probably not, but the ease with which he supplemented his skepticism with conservatism, and replaced his confidence in ideas with a confidence in custom, was indeed puzzling. Hume's individuals are halfway between Pascal's simple folk and *les demi-savants*; no longer naive, but not skeptical enough to take skepticism seriously. Whatever the merits of Hume's philosophy and the power of his arguments, he provided ammunition for *les demi-savants* who legitimately (or illegitimately) took claim to his heritage. Hume did not seem troubled by the consequences of his skepticism; one even has the feeling that sometimes he enjoyed it. This, of course, has been characteristic of most skeptics in the history of philosophy. But what made Hume exceptional was that he also had quite a strong sense of security regarding moral and political order which, from today's perspective, looks out of place.

Cynical conservatism's essential weakness was disregarded by those philosophers who cared not about the problem of self-integration, but saw its essential instability as a crucial condition of inner freedom. That there was no deep, metaphysically rooted self, did not matter. What did was the multiplicity of provisional, empirical selves whose various identities came and went throughout our lives, each being succeeded, transformed, or superimposed over another. The 19th century American philosopher, William James, claimed (as have other authors since) that our existence was episodic in character and composed of multiple identity constructs only vaguely connected to one another. They claimed custom no longer exerted the overriding power to unify those episodes, making us free to be different from what we were before, disavow our previous experience, and turn the page to make a fresh start. The plurality of selves was indeed an anthropological guarantee of inner freedom, since the individual was neither hamstrung by metaphysical constraints, nor hemmed in by custom.

But the apology for this freedom was largely illusory for the reasons already indicated: once we deprive human nature of its essential core, the question of inner freedom becomes meaningless. I cannot claim to be the author of my decisions if there is no real "I." Galen Strawson, who basically agreed with James's premise and defended the episodic character of human existence, saw this consequence clearly. A more plausible interpretation would be that instead of making intentional acts of self-creation, we are created from the outcome of decisions to which we made no essential contribution. Our episodic nature means that we constitute a series of random events in which our lives are entangled; being born in a particular place, the talents we are born with, the environment in which we are raised, our psychological and biological constitution, the fate of the community in which we live, etc. These episodes in our identity are not separate stories authored by ourselves, but rather a sequence of authorless events. Achievements and failures are therefore never entirely our own, and we can be only to be held responsible for them a limited degree.

VIOLENCE AND NOTHINGNESS

The evolution of modern philosophy gradually undermined custom and social convention—the major forces that stabilized the selfless existence–ostensibly in human individuality's defense. *Les demi-savants*, no longer satisfied by Hume's cynical conservatism, sought to liberate individuals from society's increasingly unbearable pressures as well as from the political institutions and ideas that organized and legitimized it. The hitherto existing buttresses of metaphysics, religion, and epistemology dwindled, too, in some cases crumbling altogether. Those two processes–the weakening of custom and the decline of classical metaphysics, epistemology, and Christian religion–were in some complex way interrelated.

This was an epoch-making change. Pascal, despite his doubts about the human self, still looked for hope in reason and religion. Man had been created to think. "All the dignity of man consists in thought," he wrote.[5] Science and philosophical reflection, he believed, give some limited meaning to human life. As for faith, Pascal considered it a recourse against the ultimate powerlessness of reason and the font of hope that no philosophy could provide. Full of doubts and paradoxes, ever-present in human experience, faith was the true and necessary answer to man's existential restlessness. Hence, the war on faith and religion was doomed to fail. "In truth, it is the glory of religion to have for enemies men so unreasonable," he wrote, "and their opposition to it is so little dangerous that it serves on the contrary to establish its truths."[6]

As the classical formula of "man as a being guided by reason" lost its power and attractiveness, and a growing number of "unreasonable men" rejected religious faith by denying it was a component of human experience, the sensibilities that unified and clarified life were discarded as delusion. Not that this rejection would bring true closure, but it would remove all the reasons for seeking closure at all. Once this rejection was accomplished, freedom would manifest itself as man's most primal, authentic condition, anteceding all of his social roles, diversions, experiences, and provisional identities.

Philosophically, this meant entering murky waters. This process of destruction and demystification left a person not only desolate and alien to the world around him, but also on the verge of nonbeing. "My existence was beginning to cause me some concern. Was I a mere appearance?"

asked Roquentin, the protagonist in Jean-Paul Sartre's *La Nausée*.[7] In his *Existentialism Is a Humanism*, Sartre wrote: "To begin with, [man] is nothing." On the other hand, he continued, "[Man] will not be anything until later and then he will be what he makes of himself."[8] In other words, "man is freedom" and this freedom is essentially limitless; it is freedom comparable to that of God. Man "can choose only to be God," Sartre wrote in *Being and Nothingness*. He continued: "Freedom is nothing other than a choice that creates for itself its own possibilities. [...] The initial project of being God which 'defines' man comes close to being the same as a human 'nature' or an 'essence'."[9]

So, man is nothing, and man is God. Obviously, these two extreme points of human potentiality that Sartre seemed to unite were purely theoretical constructs and were not meant to depict actual human existence. We were concrete human beings, living our lives in a concrete social and historical environment. The experience of freedom must, therefore, also be concrete. Sartre and others were well aware of this problem and had a simple answer to it. Freedom, they said, expressed itself in resolute action. The search for authenticity was a continuous radical, sometimes iconoclastic, rebellion against social and cultural constraints, against the rules, norms, and hierarchies, against philosophical systems and the ideas that established order. All of these were alien intrusions reifying and petrifying our free existence. But the rebellion was also an act of self-assertion; a realization, however imperfect, of one's godlike potentiality, a visible, albeit ephemeral, exteriorization of individual existence.

This mixture of negative and positive qualifications—freedom as a negative act of defiance and a positive manifestation of existence; a rejection and an assertion—is typical of this view of human freedom. Mersault, the loathsome protagonist in Camus's *Stranger*, for whom everything external, moral, or social was alien and uninteresting, was an extension of Sisyphus, the Greek hero who, as Camus argued in his long essay, toiled endlessly and discovered the purposelessness of his activity without falling into despair. But Mersault was also part rebel (*l'homme revolté*) a nihilist who defied the rules of injustice to live life more fully and help mankind, and to whom Camus devoted his major philosophical work. "I rebel, therefore, we exist," wrote Camus in his essay. The rebel's finite existence entertained no hope for individual or collective salvation, yet his rebellion was future-oriented and essentially altruistic: "the generosity of rebellion [...] unhesitatingly gives the strength of its love and without a moment's delay refuses injustice. Its merit lies in making no calculations, distributing everything it possesses to life and to living men. It is thus that it is prodigal in its gifts to men to come. Real generosity toward the future lies in giving all to the present," wrote Camus.[10]

Roquentin, Sartre's character from *La Nausée* (and even more loathsome than Mersault) came from the same narrative that included *Existentialism is a Humanism,* which claimed that how an individual manifested his freedom conditioned how others expressed theirs. Roquentin's nausea could mean a radical detachment from the outer world, but could also be interpreted as a vivid illustration of an extreme form of humanism. For Sartre, there must have been a clear continuity not only between *La Nausée* and *Existentialism is a Humanism,* but also between those two works and his own political involvement. As he tussled with the French police in the Paris demonstrations, dressed in a Maoist uniform, he must have believed that, at that moment, his philosophy, commitment, thoughts, and deeds were one.

Philosophers who were attracted to this view had a singular penchant for violent action, and it is easy to see why. Violence was thought to be a salient manifestation of individual freedom and of its implied "generosity." While individual violence was done for the sake of others, it was believed to be entirely free, without any collective discipline or ideological uniformity. A rebel resorting to violence was not just an ordinary party comrade (*Parteigenosse*) executing his superiors' routine orders, or a petty bureaucrat in the well-functioning, depersonalized machinery of terror, but a Stirnerian Egoist with an unbounded drive for self-realization.

The philosophers who were carried away by their belief in political violence's redeeming role denied its systemic character, even in the movements that represented the most extreme forms of party discipline and conformity. Sartre put on a Maoist uniform because he was sincerely convinced that China's Cultural Revolution, one of the most totalitarian, steered-from-above mass movements in human history, was spontaneous and sustained by a free, humanistic spirit. And Sartre was not the only one who found Marxism congenial. André Malraux, a novelist of discernible existentialist leanings, had his characters seek authenticity in revolutionary Communism, in its vehemence, violence, terror, and executions; in other words, in the extreme situations that Communist revolutions supplied in large quantities.

Camus's writings contain much violence. *L'Homme Revolté* has many long passages about the Russian nihilist terrorists who were famous, or rather notorious for, not just their readiness to shed the blood of alleged tyrants but also for accepting the consequences of their crimes with unflinching steadfastness. Camus was undoubtedly fascinated by their courageous resoluteness even in the face of death. One of those nihilist terrorists, Ivan Kaliayev, seemed to be his favorite, and Camus admired his demeanor. "Kaliayev," Camus wrote, "condemned to the gallows after having stood as prosecutor before the tribunal, declares firmly: *I consider my death as a supreme protest against a world of blood and tears*, and again: *From the moment when I found myself behind bars, I never for one moment wanted to stay alive in any way whatsoever.*"[11]

But despite long ruminations about the individualistic and nonconformist side of violence, despite tortuous arguments that were intended to explain how one could pass from Mersault to Kaliayev, or from Roquentin's sense of nonexistence to uncompromising and politically committed humanism, or from the nausea of ultimate rejection to the generosity of full involvement, the entire project was flawed. Both the negative and positive aspects of rebellion left little room for one's individuality to manifest itself. Rebellion against a particular society's oppressiveness, or in favor of some future society, became so programmed and stereotyped that it was the last place to look for radical nonconformity. In fact, rebellion soon became the very epitome of mental conformity.

Since the Enlightenment, rebelling against the status quo and being a midwife to a new era of humanism were considered the most imposing expressions of man's relationship with society. Leading cultural authorities commended or even worshipped such acts, and throngs of thoughtless imitators obediently followed them. Rebellion also had a direct influence on man's search for inner freedom, as can be seen in Marxism's spectacular progression and pervasive influence. Marxism demonstrated how one could reject the false consciousness that legitimized the prevailing order's ideas and institutions, and which was believed to squelch one's identity. It also showed how individuals could attain a greater level of self-realization by embracing the new order. This double device almost immediately transformed itself into two clichés: an inner compulsion to be militantly anti-bourgeois, anti-capitalist, anti-Christian, and anti-conservative; and an equally strong inner compulsion to side with all progressive causes, from communism, socialism, to many other -isms, which it was initially believed would wither away with the march of progress but which miraculously began to multiply with those causes' ensuing victories. Being true to one's humanity thus became the easiest thing on earth, both in terms of what one had to be for and against. The Stirnerian Egoist never materialized, but the *Parteigenosse* and petty apparatchiks of progress did, and in great quantities.

There have been attempts to dilute these clichés and turn them into something profound, mostly through verbal trickery, of the kind we encounter in the philosophy of existentialism; that is, by depicting them in a most obscure philosophical jargon, for instance, about the shades of existence or nonexistence or about the dialectical ambiguities of political commitments. An unparalleled example of this is Maurice Merleau-Ponty's long, dialectical deliberations in *Humanism and Terror*, in which he argued that the Gulag and the Moscow trials could only be properly evaluated from the perspective of the humanist order that Communism promised to build in the future.

Not surprisingly, these attempts never succeeded. The path that led from Roquentin's life on the brink of nonexistence to Sartre dressed in a Maoist uniform was neither particularly long nor curved. Nor would it have been particularly long and curved for Mersault under different circumstances. The fact that Camus opposed Communism and criticized his Communist fellow travelers was not because he was closer to Mersault, Sisyphus, or Kaliayev, but because he as a man had more honesty and decency than his colleagues.

Flirting with revolution, violence, and radicalism in the era of aggressive totalitarianism did not serve intellectuals well, including those who believed they had inscribed freedom into human existence by depriving it of its essential properties. Most of them, having filled volumes with barely comprehensible musings on how one finds one's authenticity in the omnipresent meaninglessness, ended up as ordinary fellow travelers, committed to and duped by political ideologies so crude that only a perverted mind could give them their assent. Anti-essentialism, which abolished the magnificent philosophical constructions of the past masters, turned out to be a particularly ineffective weapon against run-of-the-mill crudeness. There was nothing noble or instructive about the fall of those philosophers. Nor was there anything tragic. "Sad" or "pathetic" would be probably more accurate words to describe their story.

Their error was a fundamental one. The idea that the nonself could have a godlike creative power to develop its own authentic and existentially vibrant identities, including political ones, assumed the *creatio ex nihilo* principle that from nothing everything could emerge. But this was a most implausible claim, resembling to some extent Baron Münchausen's boastful assertion that he could pull himself out of the mire by his own pigtail. The nonself had neither means nor ends at its disposal. The nonself was nothing and, as nothing, it had nothing.

The philosophers who called for resolute action had to avail themselves of preexisting resources, and what existed were emancipatory ideologies all constructed from a few crass notions. By annihilating the self, philosophers deprived themselves of all conceptual instruments with which to combat ideologies such as Marxism that likewise, though for somewhat different reasons, undermined human nature's essential qualities and praised the creative power of political violence. No matter how hard they tried to dissent from totalitarian ideologies, they ultimately served their cause. From the perspective of the victims, as well as from that of outside observers, the difference between a Communist or a German National Socialist and a sophisticated philosopher covering up, denying, or legitimizing the crimes of totalitarian regimes for intellectually refined reasons, was negligible.

Their error had even more profound implications. Their fall refuted the belief, to which they were so attached and on which they had built their reputation, that the nonself was the condition of inner freedom. The experience of totalitarianism proved the opposite. The fact that they so naturally made advances to the most abhorrent regimes revealed their propensity for freedom to be a sham. They turned out to be gullible, other-directed, herd-like, volatile, capricious, and incongruous people, the very antithesis of those about whom we could say were true to themselves. Their opposites, people who believed in the religious and metaphysical essence of human existence, fared much better confronting totalitarian regimes. Such people courageously resisted external pressure. Their inner selves never capitulated to the temptations abounding from repressive regimes or to the terror that their henchmen ruthlessly applied to the population.

CHAPTER 12

THE MINIMAL SELF

BETWEEN FREEDOM AND NECESSITY

The next version of the self might be called minimalist. There is such a thing as the self, but it is reduced to a few simple characteristics such as utility and self-preservation. The first of these considers human nature a simple mechanism for seeking pleasure and avoiding pain; the second considers it an equally simple life preservation mechanism. In both instances, it is assumed that whatever human beings do and strive for, no matter how lofty or complex, is either a variant or a consequence of these mechanisms.

Sometimes this simple view has been slightly enriched or differently described, for example, in Hobbes's "perpetual and restless desire of power after power, that ceaseth only in Death,"[1] or in Nietzsche's "will to power." The latter biological concept was given a larger meaning in Nietzsche's positive pronouncements (made during rare moments when he forgot about his adversaries). When he was negative (that is, when he was demolishing Western philosophy) the biological meaning predominated, conjuring up blond savages, beasts of prey, wild creatures with insatiable appetites and untamable energies, especially when contrasted with the timid, fearful, weak, sick, and frustrated metaphysicians, mystics, and Christian believers.

The problem with these views of the self is fundamental and has been clearly identified. Once we assume that whatever we do, think, and aspire to is a consequence of our natural desire to survive, experience pleasure, or seek power, then the problem of inner freedom disappears. What defines our life is not the authorship of our decisions but the irresistibility of natural inclinations which we cannot but follow. The survival instinct and the mechanism of utility are at the core of humanity and cannot be sidestepped or eliminated. Whoever has a weak will to power is doomed to be a frustrated weakling, reactive, and resentful; those that have a high degree of such will are like lions, destined to dominate others.

The expression "being oneself" or "being true to oneself" becomes vacuous since, in our desire to survive, avoid pain, or endlessly seek power, we are bound by objective conditions that cannot be changed by our decisions. In more radical interpretations, human conduct resembles the movement of physical bodies and, consequently, the philosophy of man might be regarded as a type of natural science, where in place of the laws of mechanics, we have laws describing the rhythms governing human passions, desires, and instincts. Versions of this approach can be found in certain theories of economic action, sociobiology, and in interpretations of sexual behavior. In all of them, an individual might personally consider himself as acting spontaneously and solely from his own free will yet, when viewed from outside, his behavior appears highly predictable and following the objective rules of nature or the logic of human action.

"Nothing in appearances can be explained on the basis of the concept of freedom, but there the guide must always consist in the mechanism of nature," wrote Immanuel Kant in his *Critique of Practical Reason*. His example was that of a man with a "lustful inclination," and the question Kant asked was: "Whether, if in front of the house where [the man] finds this opportunity a gallows were erected on which he would be strung up immediately after gratifying his lust, he would not then conquer his inclination."[2] One might safely predict that confronted with such a gruesome alternative the man would control his lust, as fear of death would undoubtedly overcome his appetite for sexual satisfaction.

Both sexual desire and the instinct for self-preservation were said to be deeply ingrained in man's nature, and both were integral parts of his self. One, therefore, could not say that saving his life by renouncing his sexual activity was a betrayal of his self or that indulging in sexual gratification and then losing his life would have been a triumph of his authenticity. In both cases, the element of freedom was minimal because the courses of action were predetermined. The problem emerged only as a result of a clash between two natural desires, but the solution to this conflict—either in favor of sexual gratification or in favor of saving one's life—was not a matter of free choice, but of which drive turned out to be stronger, and this depended on the natural constitution of each individual.

Kant juxtaposed this situation with another scenario where the alternative was not between gratifying a lustful appetite and dying on the gallows, but between betraying a friend and facing death. The choice between whether to denounce one's friend or to refuse to do so and be punished by death (not a rare dilemma in the history of mankind) was, according to Kant, a real free and moral decision since sacrificing one's life, though the ultimate choice, could be rationally contemplated. It was certainly not automatically rejected by the instinct for self-preservation. And even if self-preservation prevailed, the choice was not obvious. One could imagine somebody deciding to save his life and being tormented to the end of his days by the pangs of conscience. Such a person might think that, when he made his choice, he was not being true to himself and that his moral self was violated.

Kant's argument is correct within the framework of his moral philosophy and within those of several others. But there is a counterargument. If we consistently uphold the concept of the minimal self and define it by self-preservation and related desires, the difference between the two situations depicted by Kant would no longer exist. Preserving one's life is an absolute priority, and in dire circumstances it must overrule all other obligations, including the bonds of friendship; if it did not, it would no longer be the essential property of the self. Therefore, there should not be any sign of conflict between that side of the person that denounced a friend and the other that was responsible for self-preservation. One is identical to the other.

A modified version of this mechanism can be observed in some of the extreme sports in which survival has been the ultimate principle, particularly in Himalayan mountaineering. The sport abounds with drastic cases: the mountaineers who are stronger usually leave their weaker colleagues behind to die whenever helping them would jeopardize their own lives. Such practices are generally accepted, including by the ethical committees that decide whether abandoning friends to die is or is not a breach of mountaineering's ethical code. And those committees hardly ever condemn such acts. It does not mean that the decision not to help a friend is considered ethical in the Kantian sense, or any other sense, but is viewed as natural, rational, and therefore admissible. The moral dilemmas of the kind mentioned by Kant very rarely appear in public debate. Even if some of the survivors feel pangs of conscience, the practice itself has never been challenged. Joseph Conrad's novel about Lord Jim, a sailor who had a moment of weakness and spent the rest of his life trying to make up for it, does not seem to have any relevance here.

In less extreme situations—that is, in our daily lives when the pressure of self-preservation or the mechanism of utility are not so direct and implacable—we are prone to making more complicated decisions, calculating short-term and long-term risks, making trade-offs, devising strategies that include satisfaction of less pressing desires, and seeking more refined pleasures. One can think of any kind of human existence, from an illiterate hoodlum to a great statesman, from an uneducated peasant to a nuclear physicist, that can be constructed or derived from such decisions and strategies. A desire for self-preservation might induce us to institute an ingenious system of efficient laws that protect our liberties and secure stable rules of cooperation. A mechanism of utility may lead us and, as John Stuart Mill maintained it often does, to high aspirations and noble goals. "It is better," wrote Mill in an often-quoted passage in his *Utilitarianism*, "to be a human being dissatisfied than a pig satisfied; better to be Socrates dissatisfied than a fool satisfied. And if the fool or the pig thinks otherwise, that is because they know only their own side of the question. The other party to the comparison knows both sides."[3]

We could envision a theory (indeed such theories are being formulated) that describes the logic of decision-making and takes into account as many factors as possible: the degree of trust towards other people; the degree of uncertainty, risk, long-term and short-term predictions; certain natural inclinations of individual human characters; the assessment of alternatives, etc. Life would resemble a complex game that people play in order to maximize utility; some to enrich themselves, some to acquire political power, others to make academic careers, still others to pursue countless different goals. For such a theory, the goals are of less importance; what matters is how one should play in order to reach the chosen objective.

But this does not bring us closer to inner freedom. We cannot say that whoever shows more skill in playing the game of life has greater inner freedom, or that his successful actions better reflect his inner self. The question is never about whether one is authentic or inauthentic, true or untrue to one's own real self, the architect of one's own life or not. Rather, the question concerns the success or otherwise of one's endeavors, of how many errors there are in one's strategy to maximize one's utility. People are perceived from the outside in the light of how they play the game, not how much inner freedom they believe they have. The question of the real self is not a factor. From the perspective of decision theory, Socrates's strategy in his game of life was a disaster, yet few could surpass him in inner freedom. Indeed, many Christian ethics must be disqualified, including "turning the other cheek" which, from the decision-theory point of view, is complete nonsense.

This discloses a more general problem. Philosophies which reduce the human self to simple characteristics that can be objectively interpreted in economic, biological, praxeological, and other theories have difficulty in distinguishing between a description and a norm. Their theories are essentially descriptive: human beings, they claim, are primarily motivated by certain objective mechanisms. There is not much room for a normative dimension. To say that people "ought to" be motivated by the desire to seek pleasure and avoid pain makes little sense because every human action is believed to be motivated by such desires. Both a pig and Socrates use their respective natures to follow these desires and neither needs outside instruction. True, we may learn to be more skillful in our actions, and these theories may be instrumental in this, but the basic mechanism is there. Whoever lacks it is not quite human or, for that matter, not quite animal. Hence, doing justice to the problem of inner freedom, or even conceiving it properly, has been endemically difficult for such theories.

The only way to introduce normative content is to modify the initial assumption. Thus, we would then say people are generally motivated by utility and self-preservation, yet are often misled by various illusions, phantoms, and idols, by bizarre creeds, irrational fantasies, wild ideologies, and unrealistic aspirations, which turn them away from their natural inclinations. Most of the calamities that have befallen the human race, be they genocide, disastrous social engineering, wars, or oppressive regimes, have resulted from quelling our instincts of utility. We would therefore be better off if we remained distrustful of those big ideas and followed our desire to preserve life, seek pleasure, and avoid pain, and to express our will to power. In our lives, we "ought to" be motivated by them.

This norm is often presented as a voice of sanity and moderation during times when people are susceptible to outbursts of uncontrolled collective enthusiasms and passions. Yet one cannot fail to notice that the norm is strongly reductionist. It compels us to reduce or, at least, to bracket larger and higher dimensions of our motivations and inspirations since they are presumed to be artificial, arbitrary, and often harmful. Though few would say that all of these dimensions should be entirely disposed of, the norm as such engenders a profound skepticism towards them. Whether from this point of view Mill's pig would win some points we do not know, but we cannot exclude the idea. Socrates, however, with his extreme and, in the eyes of many, rather dubious demands imposed on himself and others, undoubtedly would fall from the pedestal of human excellence.

This reductionism encourages us to think that the more we strip ourselves of those social, moral, religious, and other bonds and rules, the more we are ourselves. For those who believe that such bonds and rules unnecessarily regulate their sexual conduct, undermining them seems an obvious way to regain authenticity. Those who claim that economic, socio-biological, and praxeological theories adequately describe human action, usually hold the view that internalizing the logic of these theories and practicing them in real life brings liberation from the world of oppressive political or moralistic illusions in which they live. For Nietzscheans, a total debunking of classical metaphysics and Christian religion liberates their existence from the unnatural bonds of self-denial and from a belief in "an illusory higher order of things."

The minimal self, as one can see, takes a consistently anti-conservative stance, without even realizing it. It assumes that most of the impediments to human freedom–the prohibitions, taboos, and coercive misconceptions–are creations from the past that must be removed. Therefore, the past is viewed as an arena in which the real fought to liberate itself from the artificial. One can see a persistent pattern throughout history: true human motives are smothered by artificial constructs until they burst forth sporadically, often in violent revolutionary events. Nietzsche labelled this concept a "genealogy," others called the "hermeneutics of suspicion," in which culture, religion, and philosophy are understood not by what they say explicitly, but by what they unknowingly camouflage and mystify, and what interests and desires they are intended to satisfy or repress.

As a result of its inherent reductionism, the norm in question is therefore always directed against the status quo and its historical and philosophical foundations in the widest possible sense. To a varying degree, it always tends to simplify complexity, flatten hierarchies, truncate that which is too ornamental and ramified, and downsize what is not useful. By chopping off what's unnecessary and harmful, it is believed human beings will arrive at a longed-for state in which they are finally their true selves and not what others want them to be.

Oftentimes this pruning has been quite substantial. The champions of the sexual revolution made devastating incursions into social practices, morality, culture, and politics, dramatically changing the world in which we live by liquidating a complex system of obligations and inhibitions that had been built over centuries to tame human sexuality. In their herme-neutics of suspicion, Nietzsche reduced Western metaphysics to a form of disease; Freud reduced it to sex, the unconscious, the death drive and various ways of coping with them. Both writers, as well as their numerous followers, propagated the clearly internally inconsistent view that the distinction between the high and the low–the sublime and the vulgar–which for many centuries had dominated how human life was perceived, made no sense. What defined human life for them was the low and the vulgar rather than the high and the sublime.

In addition, the market logic of capitalism was seen as a bulldozer that wiped out the rich fabric of medieval society. Its destructive power was so great that even Marx and Engels could not conceal their admiration and envy. Capitalism, they wrote, "has pitilessly torn asunder the motley feudal ties that bound man to his *natural superiors*, and has left remaining no other nexus between man and man than naked self-interest than cal-lous *cash payment*. It has drowned the most heavenly ecstasies of religious fervor, of chivalrous enthusiasm, of philistine sentimentalism, in the icy water of egotistical calculation. [...] It has been the first to show what man's activity can bring about. It has accomplished wonders far surpassing Egyptian pyramids, Roman aqueducts, and Gothic cathedrals."[4] Even if Marx and Engels's remarks seem somewhat excessive, one can find similar, less poetic and more precise descriptions in Max Weber's writings.

The growth of liberalism across Western civilizations had a similar effect. Although, in theory and practice, liberalism did not recreate the type of austere society described by Hobbes and Locke, it nevertheless considerably influenced its structure and societal mores. To the extent that their society resembled the liberal model, it also illustrated the functioning of the norm in question. Liberalism stimulated the process of stripping our social life and ourselves of many elements along the lines that liberal philosophy had envisaged. It had its share, for example, in pushing society towards individualism, in which a collection of self-contained agents collaborated through contracts, akin to liberal philosophy's social order. We are closer to this order today than ever before.

It does not require much perceptiveness to see that the norm—people ought to be motivated by utility, self-preservation, will to power, a sense of womanhood (in the case of women), a strong homosexual preference, etc.—does not solve the problem it was meant to solve. Instead of giving us the freedom to be ourselves, the norm draws us into dependence. It tells us that whenever we deviate from theoretical models, for instance whenever we do not maximize utility or follow market logic, we are mistaken, deluded, or uninformed. Therefore, we must behave in the rational or natural manner proscribed by whatever theory in order to be rational, natural, and human. Only by subjecting ourselves to these theoretical sexual, economic, or political directives will we acquire inner freedom.

All of this creates a most peculiar mindset. On the one hand, it is characterized by a sincere yearning to be able to speak in one's own voice and express one's own opinions; but, on the other, there is an almost thoughtless acceptance of a very concrete blueprint of what it means to be authentic. Being authentic usually means assuming an anti-conservative stance that enables one to throw off or suspend a lot of the social, moral, religious, and philosophical constructs and conventions that Western civilization has created over many centuries. It also allows one to identify oneself with all that is simple, real, and direct, functional and average, body-related, self-interested, self-satisfied, and instinctual. Since these factors, either individually or combined, make it possible to give a more or less objective account of human behavior, those who choose them as primary motivations therefore follow a common pattern which is not really their own.

THE DECEPTIONS OF THE MINIMAL SELF

The conclusion that follows from the preceding remarks is that for the minimal self, inner freedom is difficult to achieve because the instruments it has at its disposal are too weak to prevent it from falling into dependency on either nature or assorted necessities and conformities. There is very little in the minimal spirit that could be called its own.

This is not an original thought. In *Phenomenology of Spirit*, Hegel arrived at a similar diagnosis which he called "disrupted consciousness." Similarly, it was exemplified by Denis Diderot's philosophical conversation *Rameau's Nephew*, in which the famous composer's nephew knew he was mediocre and would never attain the status of a genius, artist, or outstanding person, and this awareness made him bitter. However, he was good at imitating artists and geniuses, and was for a time able to impress others. But everything he did was an imitation and there was nothing of value that was his own or sprung forth from his real self.

Hegel described "disrupted consciousness" using such words as "deception," "perversion," and "shamelessness." All of them inferred its impotence, limitations, and the fictitiousness of self-identification. "If it gets beyond speaking in monosyllables, it says the same thing that is said by the educated mind, but in doing so also commits the folly of imagining it is saying something new and different," wrote Hegel. "It perverts in its speech all that is unequivocal because what is self-identical is only an abstraction, but in its actual existence is in its own self a perversion."[5]

Hegel's "disrupted consciousness" is reminiscent of Plato's democratic man from Book VIII of *The Republic of Plato*, who had a "youthful" soul that believed anything was possible, just as a young man imagines he can become whatever he likes in the future. Thus, the democratic man played a variety of roles one after another and took pleasure in such identity experiments. Such a man, as Plato said in a well-known passage, "lives along day by day, gratifying the desire that occurs to him, at one time drinking and listening to the flute, at another downing water and reducing; now practicing gymnastic, and again idling and neglecting everything; and sometimes spending his time as though he were occupied with philosophy. Often, he engages in politics and, jumping up, says and does whatever chances come to him; and if he ever admires any soldiers, he turns in that direction and if it's money-makers, in that one. And there is neither order nor necessity in his life."[6]

Hegel accurately observed that modern man had an abstract sense of self-identity; he wanted to be united internally, but felt he could not be. If faced with Kant's dilemma–to preserve his own life or denounce a friend–he would have made it a moral issue to the extent to which his abstract notion influenced his conduct, and to the extent he would have made a conscious effort to live by this notion. But the more his self was disrupted, the more he would have diluted its moral aspect by focusing on the various roles he had adopted in life. Denouncing a friend could have been one episode among many, like the democratic man who jumped from one occupation to another. The denunciation would have created a sense of guilt, remorse, and a need for atonement, but it would have been treated as an unpleasant accident caused by external circumstances, unrelated to the preceding and subsequent phases of his life.

This abstract notion of the self, that mostly flickered on the outer limits of the disrupted consciousness's intellectual horizon, was not always so remote. In fact, sometimes it was quite close. Certainly, by being too dependent on the body and its cravings, modern man had to follow its necessities and be an object rather than a subject of objective forces. But he was not just a body. In classical liberalism, for example, he also had a soul, and this abstract sense of unity derived in large part from it. If there was some philosophical space within which early modern political theory, including liberalism, could conceive of inner freedom, it was precisely the concept of the soul.

This concept was, of course, much weaker than in ancient and medieval philosophy. It was incorporated in a somewhat simplified form into political theory and Protestant theology, though it soon decoupled from its original source. The individualism that developed during early modernity hinged as much on the human body, with its natural inclination to seek pleasure and avoid pain, as it did on the unique experience of faith. Individuals might have resembled Rameau's nephew or Plato's democratic man in the artificiality of what they were doing, yet whenever they examined their religious consciousness, they discovered that they were unified by sharing one soul but still distinct from everyone else. Faith and salvation were entirely individual.

This view exerted a strong influence on societies that were moving towards a liberal order and provided them with what they lacked; namely, diversity. A liberal society composed of minimal selves, as depicted by Locke and others, was rather arid, gray, largely uninspiring, and centered almost solely on property and its derivatives. Such a world was totally unlike those later fantasies of a free society that was profoundly diverse, colorful, full of eccentrics and geniuses, and effervescing with human creativity and individual initiatives. What provided this lackluster collection of hardworking men with color and multifariousness was the variety of individual souls, each having a unique religious identity of remarkable strength and cohesion. Therefore, each individual could claim that, contrary to Hegel, his consciousness was not disrupted and, contrary to Plato, his daily occupations did not deprive his life of autonomous unity.

The basis of this view was St. Paul's distinction between the inner and outer man, which can be found in Romans 7:22-23. "I joyfully concur with the law of God in the inner man," wrote St. Paul, "but I see a different law in the members of my body." Whereas medieval Christian rationalism and the Catholic Church in various, often complex ways, reduced the tension between the inner and outer man, as well as between the realms of faith and reason, Protestants tended to treat both as being autonomous.

The problem then arose of how the inner and outer man should cooperate with each other. Ideally, the outer man, like his neighbors, followed existing laws, the rules of the market, and the way of the flesh, but his inner self was free and undisturbed. The objective world could make him perform various roles, but this did not affect his internal identity. That was an obvious consequence of St. Paul's words. In practice, however, the handling of outer religion and the inner man became a serious political problem. Outer religion was seen as a force through which inner man's dangerous "enthusiasms" or, as Locke put it in his *Letter Concerning Toleration*, his "burning zeal for God" could destabilize political order and even create civil wars.[7] Religion was believed to be the single most divisive factor in political life; therefore, keeping it in check was one of government's primary duties.

The proposed solution, which once institutionalized had an enormous influence on the modern world, was the separation of church and state. In real terms, at least in Europe (America was a different story), this translated into the subjection of churches to the state, and of religion to politics. When the political sovereign becomes the head of the church, one can hardly call such an arrangement the separation of religion and politics. Wherever this happened, outer religion and outer man were controlled, or at least carefully watched, while inner man and inner religion, though theoretically absolutely free, gradually receded into the deepest areas of human subjectivity.

Of particular significance was the argument that pushed this process even further: since the government controlled the church, it was a fundamental civic duty to obey the state and its laws, even when that meant disobeying religious duties—something inner man found objectionable and sinful. Government could be regarded as the supreme pontiff, not ensuring the salvation of people's souls but rather their physical peace. Additionally, government had the power to invalidate all religious objections to society's rules, deeming the latter beneficial to the common good. When a man "is subject to no civil law," wrote Hobbes, "sinneth in all he does against his conscience, yet it is not so with him that lives in a commonwealth; because the law is the public conscience, by which he had already undertaken to be guided. Otherwise in such diversity, as there is of private consciences, which are but private opinions, the commonwealth must needs be distracted."[8]

State control of the church took many forms, applying varying degrees of strictness, sometimes selectively. Generally, this new relationship between faith and politics (and, consequently, between the sacred and the profane) contributed to secularization's growth. From the outset, it became obvious that the altar was inferior to the throne and could not oppose it. This relationship was different in Catholic countries, where, depending upon the state, the process of secularization had a more complex and sometimes more violent character.

In societies that attempted to follow the liberal model, this arrangement ultimately led to religion becoming internalized. This effect could be seen even in non-Protestant countries. Inner man became the only politically acceptable religious being and the more hidden he was the better. By the same token, an increasing number of actions, opinions, and forms of expression started to be counted as an outer religion, and as such subject to increasing pressure from political rules and legal regulations. The concept of "separation" turned into "neutrality of the state." More recently, this neutrality has evolved into a powerful bureaucratic machine that has tracked down and eliminated all symbols and signs which might be regarded as inner man's intrusion into the public realm.

This machine has acquired a dynamic of its own, fueled by its internal logic, but has also been eagerly applauded by militant secularists and acquiesced to by those Christians who have felt compelled to join the tide of modernity. To achieve the neutrality of the state it has been necessary to separate—or rather sever off from it—everything that could be perceived as having a relationship to religion. Having been started, the process appears to have no end. The cleansing of such elements from the public space has only accelerated. In recent years, the mere visibility of crucifixes, the Nativity, the ten commandments, or a holy medal has been deemed a violation of the state's neutrality. While inner man's existence has been acknowledged, albeit reluctantly, he is expected not to identify himself publicly as such. Athletes who make the sign of the cross after scoring a goal or before starting a race are one such example.

When Locke wrote his *Letter Concerning Toleration*, he never doubted that religion and morality were intertwined. Religious communities therefore should be responsible for their members' moral formation and inculcating them with virtue. That was presumably the legacy of the old way of thinking that he somehow retained. Alternatively, Locke used this strategy to convince readers that, as he understood it, religious toleration left society's moral mechanisms and principles untouched. For a long time, Locke's conviction was largely shared. But once government involved itself in morality and began legislating on matters of life and death, first in totalitarian systems, then more recently in liberal democracies, those mechanisms and principles stood in modernity's way and had to be removed. No wonder Hobbes's concept that the law was the public conscience's invalidation of the private conscience look on a new life.

Perhaps the most momentous instance of this has been the elimination of conscience clauses from the legal system in many European countries, which for years have protected doctors, priests, and people in many other professions and occupations. If there were a perfect illustration of today's application of Hobbes's device, this would be it. The elimination of conscience clauses has gone almost unnoticed and largely unopposed. It has been performed in a matter-of-fact way like a routine technical operation, without controversy, and tacitly approved by the vast majority. Although no one has talked about inner man and outer religion, these concepts have been clearly implied. In this case however, the conscience, whether relating to abortion or euthanasia, has been assumed to be a direct product of outer religion and therefore considered negligible.

Some might find it puzzling how easily modernity has transitioned from the view that the conscience was the core of human individuality and thus sacred, to a widespread belief that violating it was absolutely justifiable. But looking back at the arguments that intellectually organized modernity and constituted a modern concept of man, one should not be surprised. Since the political power of the *regio* has always had a superior authority over *religio*, the abolition of conscience clauses had to happen as a matter of course. Since today there is *una regio*–and modern liberal democracy is such *una regio*–there cannot be but *una religio*, and it does not matter that this *religio* is an anti-Christian, secular ideology.

After this ideology disqualified religion, first in its outer form then relegating it to the dustbin of history, the dismissal of anything related to religion, including an individual conscience, was in a way logical. Hobbes and others argued that by imposing an outer religion, the state left individuals with a large space in their soul in which they could, and should, find spiritual satisfaction. But with the rejection of religion, articulating a similar argument today sounds utterly disingenuous. This erstwhile infinite space within the soul has ceased to exist.

This is no trifling matter, since it has so easily allowed for systemic, brutal encroachments on people's freedom. One might wonder what will replace the soul's function as the carrier of one's inner freedom, now that it has been deprived of its religious essence? From what source can one derive unmistakable certainty that one's actions, convictions, and attitudes are really one's own while others are not?

The answer is that there is no such source because the very idea that human nature contains something profound enough to be that source has been eliminated. The abolition of the distinction between profound and superficial brings us back to the point from which we started; that is, we are once more in Hegel's situation of "disrupted consciousness." We are back to Rameau's nephew and Plato's democratic man with their various performances and roles, none of which are authentic and none can claim superiority over others. Modern man has lost whatever chance he had of justifying his aspiration to authenticity. The aspiration remains–in fact, his hunger to be himself has increased–but there is nothing left at his disposal with which he could justify his claim and satisfy his need.

The place vacated by the soul has been captured by various temporary occupations that attract one's attention and for a while seem to constitute one's identity, just as in Plato's democratic man. They may come from prevailing ideologies, or mass culture, fashions, or other external sources, and are often eagerly absorbed as a long-desired vehicle of authenticity, but usually, are soon abandoned as worthless. Some are ambitious, some are not; some are grotesque; but all of them are considered equally valid. To question this equal validity would be considered hurtful and cruel to the people who passionately desire to be themselves, each of them in their own unique way. One may wonder the provenance of such sensitivity in a society that has had no qualms in outlawing moral conscience and has ruthlessly imposed its political rule over the moral interpretation of life and death. Upon reflection, one may come to the conclusion that this sensitivity cannot be authentic.

CHAPTER 13

A STRONG CONCEPT OF SELF

THE POLITICAL MAN

The concept of the minimal self, which today is having its heyday since it is held to be the only acceptable view of human nature, was until relatively recently never at the center of Western philosophical tradition. Ancient Greek philosophy devoted much more space and attention to a more robust view of human nature which was developed in the Middle Ages and later continued in some currents of modernity. The reason why this strong view predominated is obvious. Contrary to the individualist theories, human societies have never been simply collections of self-contained, isolated individuals, but have been perceived as consisting of beings with larger social, historical, ethnic, and religious identities. Reducing society to a collection of individuals is something we can envisage as a thought experiment or something that might come about in reality, but only through intense social engineering or social disintegration.

One can find compelling proof that this more densely complex view better describes human nature, even in existing societies that call themselves individualistic and openly laud the concept of the minimal self. More than others, these societies have been a fertile ground for often radically transformational political ideologies that have supplied seemingly independent and self-constituting individuals with a general sense of purpose and collective identity. Today's Western societies are a case in point. Rampant with radical, collectivist ideologies built along racial, sexual, and ethnic lines, they leave less and less room for nonideological activity and thinking. Although these identities are artificial (that is, not derived from genuine historical experience but rather a surrogate of the real thing) the fact that they have been in demand demonstrates something important about human nature. Despite philosophical fantasizing about self-sufficient individuals, human beings need a deep sense of belonging and the more they are individualized, the more they are eager to assimilate collective identities–even absurd ones–without realizing to what extent their self-proclaimed individual sovereignty is illusory.

Aristotle was the first thinker who defined a human being in his social and historical dimension, using the expression "political man," the adjective "political" referring initially to the Greek *polis* (city-state), and later to a state as it came to be understood in the modern era. For Aristotle, "man is a political being" was primarily an empirical statement: no other free man lived in a Greek *polis*. But Aristotle also formulated a philosophical argument: human beings were essentially political, he claimed, because they could evolve and thrive only as a part of communities which provided them with a moral and political education, and, consequently, with all the skills necessary to develop human nature. These skills (the Greeks called them "virtues") were a mark and a criterion of how successful people were in their humanity.

Since one of the constituents of the city-state was the family, or what Aristotle called the household, it was obvious that whoever did not set up a household, get married, or have children was not fully human, or at least lacked those certain qualities which one could master only by performing one's familial duties. Similarly, those who did not participate in the *kome* (a small agrarian community) lacked certain skills. Most importantly, those who did not act as citizens in a city-state could not develop the qualities needed to acquire those necessary virtues.

The above completely changes the perspective through which one perceives inner freedom. Until now, talking about inner freedom of the nonexistent or minimal selves implied searching for a mode of existence that was claimed to be suppressed by various allegedly imposed loyalties. To be true to oneself or, at least, not to be untrue to oneself, meant reflecting on one's life and one's decisions to find something that was untouched by external influences. With the political man, it is different. The question is: how much of my humanity have I been able to activate and what skills have I acquired to develop my human potential? In other words, enlarging one's freedom does not mean getting rid of various social roles and taking off various social costumes but, on the contrary, accepting these roles and costumes to gain the necessary competencies that they require.

One can think of inner freedom not through the analogy of a person who gets rid of an unnecessary burden and who, having jettisoned all the heavy objects he has been ordered to carry, feels free; but rather by the analogy of a musical virtuoso who knows he must follow certain rules, but who only after having mastered those rules can achieve perfection in expressing his unique style and interpretation. Abolishing those rules or tampering too much with them would disqualify the artist rather than allow him to excel. The uniqueness of individual style and interpretation comes to the fore after years of practice; humility more than hubris is the proper approach.

It is obvious which of the following two artists—one well-trained in the art of performing, the other neglectful of it—would have more inner liberty. Which one could better and more accurately express his own emotions and sensibilities when interpreting a work of art and instill it with his inimitable personality? We would not hesitate to call the first one a better artist; neither would we hesitate in calling the second one a lesser artist.

The more one thinks of virtues such as prudence, justice, or courage, the more their analogy to artistic performances becomes apparent. One acquires these virtues gradually by acting prudently, justly, or bravely, and even when one falls short or perhaps stumbles, this should always be a lesson, just like an unsuccessful musical performance might be a lesson for a pianist. One learns to be prudent, just, or brave by years of practice, following certain rules that determine those virtues. Yet every one of those acts is always individual, imprinted with a particular set of personal experiences and circumstances. The situations which require a prudent, just, or brave action are different every time and how they are assessed may vary depending on who makes whichever decision, and why.

The political man who cares about his inner freedom will be a diligent learner, just like the person who wants to be an accomplished pianist or violinist. Whoever says: "I will not be brave," or "I do not care about justice," or "I despise family obligations," or "I will never defend my country," performs an act of moral and existential self-mutilation. It is like a musically adept person declaring his reticence to practice music and disobeying his teacher's instructions from the outset. To make a more vivid comparison: making contemptuous declarations about the virtues is like saying that to control oneself better, one would have to cut off certain limbs or refuse to walk or speak.

One may wonder from where the temptation to indulge in such pronouncements comes. Probably, they get their inspiration from the philosophy of the minimal self or the nonexistent self. However, as we have seen, the minimal or nonexistent self has little to offer: neither happiness, nor prosperity, nor great achievement. If the young pianist refuses to subject himself to the demanding process of musical education, it is clear he shuts himself down to the prospect of any serious musical career, hoping probably for some easier but sufficiently profitable occupation in popular music or some other commercial enterprise. A person who renounces the political man's duties can entertain comparable though lower hopes, but he must considerably reduce his ambition to retain his inner freedom.

The sole motive in rejecting a strong concept of the self and belittling the role of virtues and duties is a negative one. Liberal philosophy generated an incessant compulsion to rebel against everything that allegedly blocked individual genius's free expression. John Stuart Mill went quite far down this road. Having been indirectly influenced by German Romanticism and its vision of a powerful individual self, he drew a rather simple-minded conclusion that it was enough to be eccentric, or a "dissentient" as he described it, to meet the necessary conditions for becoming a free and creative spirit. But, as could have been predicted, once eccentricity became the fashion or the norm, it unleashed a wave of collectivism, not creativity. Throngs of self-proclaimed eccentrics shouting the same slogans against every form of real or imagined *ancien régimes* have always made a rather depressing spectacle of human conformity, and bear no trace of the individual geniuses that Mill had anticipated with such certainty.

The negative impulse set in motion by the liberal order admittedly has turned out to be a powerful force. It has generated an almost inexhaustible energy that fuels constant rebellions against one and the same enemy which disguises itself in ever-changing costumes. Simultaneously, it has created a stifling orthodoxy that does not tolerate dissenters and almost annihilates internal criticism or the free movement of ideas. The belief that permanent rebellion against conservative forces is not only morally right and intellectually sound, but also liberates us from false gods and identities has turned into a dogma that few dare to defy. Like Marx's concept of the class struggle, it has been employed as a key to all areas of life from literature and art, to morality and law.

It is therefore hardly surprising that in the liberal order individuality and inner freedom are rare commodities, typically viewed with hostility. The road to them leads through a different view of human nature. Virtues such as courage, prudence, justice, piety, and self-control have an unmistakable touch of individuality since they are so demanding and require great effort and strength of character. Their opposites—cowardice, recklessness, injustice, godlessness, and immoderation—are herd-like qualities. All cowards are the same, and whatever the differences among them do not count. Again, an analogy with art seems to be strikingly accurate. Great virtuosos are different, whereas inferior artists are pretty much the same and no one really cares whether one of them may be any less inferior than another.

Aristotle's view that man identified himself with the city-state had to be modified for the modern world. Since Greek city-states ceased to exist many centuries ago and all subsequent attempts to recreate them failed, the nation-state became the obvious new object of political identification and civic education. Certainly empires existed, but it was the nation-state that arrested the imagination and dominated major trends in political theory. It brought with it a strong attachment to a particular country, its traditions, and its identity.

Since antiquity, it had been recognized that nations and large ethnic groups had their own distinct identity, and this fact was considered crucial in many respects. The Athenians differed from the Spartans and, according to Thucydides, that difference influenced both the course and the aftermath of the Peloponnesian war. Modernity more forcefully articulated this idea as it developed and added certain new elements to it, such as placing greater emphasis on how language affected national identity. The concept of "culture," which spread rapidly once conceived, conveyed the complex makeup of a nation's singular distinctiveness.

Both ancient and modern versions of the concept of national identity referred to something that was a part of everyone's experience: national differences and identities were easily observable and impossible to deny. To what extent those "cultures" could be changed and were responsive to political engineering was an open question. But it was clear that they proved to have remarkable resilience to external pressure, even to ruthlessly repressive measures meted out by domestic tyrants and foreign occupiers.

Critics, however, always claimed these identities were not real; that they were mythical, artificial, contrived, superficial, and imagined, and their demise would come sooner rather than later. According to these critics, a sense of national identity led people astray into a fantasy world, one that paralyzed their will and their minds, and occasionally ignited within them a crusading spirit against other nations they considered wicked and contemptible and, as such, a threat to their own identity.

In such a formulation, the anti-nation argument is void. National identities have not disappeared and are unlikely to do so. The nation-state, in spite of broader tendencies towards globalization, has retained its dominant position. People continue to need a community that naturally unites them through a common language, history, social practices, and is cemented by loyalty, love, and even sometimes by the ultimate sacrifice.

On the other hand, it must be admitted that nationalism may have a certain flimsiness which, though convenient, can be misleading. Convenient in the sense that it provides a safe cover for one's collective identity without having any obligations. Millions of people consider themselves Polish, Swedish, Hungarian, French, etc., without a moment's reflection on what that really means and without being involved in how their country's run. Populations have no need for nationalism during stable eras but, in times of crises, silly notions may be fed into complacent minds and prompt irresponsible conduct under the pretense of serving one's country.

Throughout human history, dictators have cynically used nationalist phraseology to advance policies that were detrimental to their own nations. Romania's Communist leaders, for example, were clearly nationalistic but this did not make life easier for Romanian citizens, nor did it increase their sense of belonging to their own culture. This lack of authenticity was as harrowing and pervasive across all other Communist countries, even those that ostentatiously shunned nationalist rhetoric.

Today, the question is therefore not whether nations will survive in the age of globalization and global ideologies—they surely will—but whether they will be able to exert a creative influence on human life. Liberalism is the most powerful ideology in the Western world and has been adopted by both governments and international institutions such as the European Union. Much depends on how national cultures and global liberalism interact. Today, we are witnessing two simultaneous tendencies. There is a growing dissatisfaction with supranational institutions, particularly the EU, as they are considered notorious for their arrogance, heavy-handedness, and inefficiency. Nevertheless, liberal ideology continues its conquest of Western societies, penetrating every nook and cranny of our existence.

The United Kingdom is a case in point. Depending on one's political persuasion, Brexit has been hailed (or denounced) as a victory of nationalism over Europeanism. But at the same time, British society and its institutions are second to none in their liberal intransigence. Every single element of the liberal monopoly is there: political correctness is in full swing, secularism is rampant, legal regulations are intrusive, dissent is discriminated against, and human rights ideology has gone berserk. But the conflict between the UK and the EU has not been about these issues. Therefore, it does not seem likely that leaving the EU will make much difference to liberalism's influence. The same goes for Switzerland and Norway, neither of which have ever been members of the EU, yet both have duly kept pace with all the liberal dogmas. One can envisage a situation where more nation-states emancipate themselves from their entanglements with supranational institutions, but liberal ideology continues to tighten its grip over people's minds and souls. At which point, Aristotle's political man will be even harder to find.

THE DEPOSED KING

Defining the human self by its metaphysical dimension is another long-held belief in the West. Man, in other words, is a *homo metaphysicus*, not a frequently used term in philosophy but quite adequate in this context. The word metaphysics has never had a precise meaning but let us use it in the sense that Aristotle did, though he never actually used the word itself. Metaphysics is a philosophical inquiry into ultimate principles and causes. Taking this definition as a general framework, we could say that *homo metaphysicus* defines himself by his natural inclination to search for the ultimate meaning to both the world around him and his life. Though painfully aware of his own existence's finite and contingent nature, he nevertheless can perceive the infinite horizon and believes there might be a path that might lead him to the absolute whether through philosophy, religion, or some other means.

Metaphysical man is driven by the pervasive conviction that the goal of his existence transcends physical and societal limitations and though beyond his immediate grasp, it will determine his destiny. Even the miseries that result from his finite nature, the failures, the fragility of life, the fear of death, point in this direction. "They are," as Pascal put it, "the miseries of a great lord, of a deposed king."[1] Like a dethroned king, *homo metaphysicus* knows that there is more to his being than the imperatives of everyday life and he deems, sometimes unconsciously, his real status as being higher than the pitiful condition that his existence would indicate.

Metaphysics is most clearly represented by contrasting the finite with the infinite, or the contingent with the absolute. Everything, including life itself, is contingent and finite: our coming into existence, our survival and our demise, our suffering and our happiness. All of them bear the marks of chance and transience. Yet we know that this condition describes only a part of what we are as human beings. The human mind has a profound awareness of perfection, of completeness, of the ultimate and the absolute, and the search for these is also a search for our true identity.

Living is a constant process of making sense of what's finite in the light of what's infinite, and of what's contingent in the light of what's absolute. There might be a lot of mystification and game-playing in this process, but we all know that this is possibly the most serious matter in our existence, even if we abandon it out of despair, thoughtless defiance, or boredom. Human life therefore resembles (or should resemble despite what unforeseen chaos might prevail) a road to understanding. Since this knowledge comes from relating our existence to something higher, it has been visualized as a road leading upward towards a state of mind that reconciles the contingent with the absolute, and even overcomes its finite status. Whoever refuses to take this road loses a part of his identity; he is less himself.

The upward-road scenario is rooted in religion, especially in Christianity which emphasizes the possibility of salvation. The word "salvation" has both a metaphysical and a religious sense. It is metaphysical because it assumes a philosophical framework in a search for the "ultimate principles and causes." But it is primarily religious because it focuses on the destiny of an individual soul which through God's miraculous omnipotence can be redeemed, cleansed from its earthly sins, and transferred to the divine reality to enjoy eternal bliss. For many centuries, both the philosophical and religious perspectives were considered closely related. Whether this relationship was historical rather than substantive is an open question. One cannot fail to notice, however, that their separation coincided with the rise of secularization, which could indicate a rather deep affinity between the two.

The cave allegory from Plato's *Republic VII* contains a particularly persuasive description of *homo metaphysicus*. This is arguably the most important allegory in all of Western culture and the key to comprehending its basic metaphysical and religious dramaturgy. It claims that two dispositions define the essence of Western culture. First, we believe that the world is not self-explanatory; its meaning is hidden and has to be gradually disclosed through a long and arduous process. Second, the search for truth leads to enlightenment which opens our minds to higher things, completely changing us and how we see the world. Plato described this process as a journey that takes us from low (the cave) to high (the sun).

Plato identified this journey's lowest and highest stages as, respectively, enslavement and freedom. Initially, we see people who have lived their entire life in chains. Eventually, we encounter one man who shakes his chains off, leaves the dark cave, and finds his way to the outside world where he sees the sunlight. At last, the man can see the world as it is and his mind is freed from distorted images.

These two stages are identified in other ways: being in the cave is referred to as uneducated (*apaideusia*); being outside the cave is called educated (*paideia*). This language raises many questions. Plato considered the overwhelming majority of mankind to be men in chains, therefore this would imply that most of humanity was uneducated. Such a conclusion is all the more surprising because Plato's men in chains were not at all ignorant. Their perception of the world was coherent, rational, and true within its limits. Suffice it to say, they were able to find order in the events they observed and make accurate predictions. Still, despite its partial validity, Plato called such a state of the mind *apaideusia*.

To answer the question partially, Plato's chains symbolized a rather common intellectual state that categorically precluded metaphysical inquiry. It is noteworthy that while Plato's narrative was intended to elevate human existence by disclosing man's natural desire to find metaphysical truth, a good part of it was devoted to mankind's powerful, inherent opposition to metaphysics.

Plato was not alone in making this point. Christianity preserved this paradox, contrary to the popular perception that it was consistently egalitarian. Human nature could achieve a higher status, yet the Gospels often stressed that many people were blind and deaf to this calling. "Many are called, but few chosen," as Jesus put it Himself, in one of His most enigmatic sayings (Mat. 22:14). The saying came from the parable of the marriage feast (which symbolized the Kingdom of Heaven) given by the king, who represented God. Many refused to attend this feast, some of those who did were not properly attired, while others decided to kill the king's servants.

Whatever this parable's ultimate meaning, it nevertheless highlighted people's resistance to God's offerings even if, like the marriage feast, they were exceptionally generous. From the very beginning of Christianity, the idea that something about human nature prevented people from accepting God's wisdom has persisted, no matter that Jesus sacrificed His earthly life to save humanity, or that salvation was achievable.

This paradox disclosed the rather ambiguous position of homo metaphysicus in society. On the one hand, he was met by an intense aversion. In Plato's story, the men in chains decided to kill the man who, having found his way out of the cave, returned to it to force them to embark on the same journey. Killings featured in the parable of the feast, too. Both narratives were written from the metaphysical man's perspective, yet both depicted a violent rejection of metaphysics as well as a disdain for those who defended it.

What Plato and the Scriptures said was accurate. The hostile reaction against *homo metaphysicus* recurred throughout Western history and was reflected in philosophy, too. In antiquity, Thrasymachus's and Callicles's vituperative remarks about Socrates's "just man," who roamed around the world of intellectual fantasy seemingly oblivious of common men's natural reactions, reflected such an attitude. In early modernity, both the religious and philosophical versions of Protestantism indulged in a particularly fiery impulse to castigate ancient and medieval metaphysics as well as the Roman Catholic religion, which was said to be imbued with its spirit. In later modernity, the spread of atheism reinforced the enmity towards metaphysical man. When one reads the vast body of antimetaphysical literature spanning Thomas Hobbes to Bertrand Russell (not to mention the books of today's fanatical atheists), one easily detects the authors' angry impatience at what they consider the stubborn presence of something that should have disappeared long ago.

Using Plato's metaphor, one can say that the men in chains not only refuse to admit they are in chains but want to destroy every possible perspective from which their chains can be seen. By eliminating such perspectives, the cave becomes the entire world and their point of view the only legitimate one. Whoever disagrees and begins ruminating on the possibility of some transcendent fulfillment of human existence, or on being created in God's image, is diagnosed as suffering from delusion or a serious health defect. Nietzsche, with his usual brutality, maintained that skin and gastric diseases lay at the root of metaphysics. Others determined that metaphysics and religion grew out of a fear of the unknown to compensate for the sense of helplessness brought on by fear itself.

On the other hand, *homo metaphysicus* was at the heart of the enormous influence that metaphysics has had on Western culture. Plato, and so many after him, complained about the majority of mankind's metaphysical deafness, and the Scriptures predicted that "the subjects of the kingdom will be thrown outside, into the darkness, where there will be weeping and gnashing of teeth," (Mat. 8:12). But the metaphysical man had a strong and clearly visible presence in the public arena, in the language used, in school curricula, in art, in popular stereotypes, as well as many other places. What the metaphysical man said and aspired to became a central part of Western civilization.

Metaphysics was the ultimate anchor of vertical thinking which accepted Plato's metaphor of the journey from low to high. What was spiritual was more valued than what was material, even though the majority of mankind did not follow this precept in practice. "The spirit is willing, but the flesh is weak," as Jesus said to Peter in the Garden of Gethsemane (Mat. 26:41), and this explained the constant tension between what people professed and what they did. This also explained the power of hypocrisy as "the homage that vice pays to virtue," as well as the persistent suspicion of hypocrisy towards those who seemed to be considerably more advanced in their upward journey than most.

But a sense of hierarchy was there. Even those who did not make much progress in that journey, or failed, were aware that the human world was hierarchical: they lived, thought, and dreamed in the shadow of metaphysics. An enormous part of Western art was about metaphysics, starting in antiquity, then through the Middle Ages, and extending into some trends in Modernity. Ascension and descent, truth that liberated and falsehood that enslaved, good and evil, perfection and debasement, God and Satan, sainthood and sin, redemption and atonement, the life of the spirit and the life of the flesh. Inspired by ancient and Christian imagery, these were the subjects taken up by religious and secular art. In philosophy, ancient Greek metaphysics lived on for many centuries in European thought, influencing ethics, aesthetics, and anthropology.

With that in mind, we can see why the defenders of metaphysics could, following Plato, associate being in the cave (or its equivalent) with *apaideusia*, and exiting the cave with *paideia*. With the disappearance of *homo metaphysicus*, a large part of Western culture was bound to lose its relevance and legibility. In this new post-metaphysical world, metaphysics may become an intellectual exercise within some university philosophy and logic departments, and religion may try to prove its social usefulness by imitating psychotherapy, but both are believed to be waning irretrievably.

Considering that the metaphysical man animated classical, medieval, and a good part of modern culture, all of which documented his hopes and fears and articulated and ennobled his experience, his delegitimization over the past few centuries has practically annihilated this enormous output of human genius and debunked the impressive results from its wrestle with the ultimate. The human horizon has begun to resemble that of the pre-Platonic and pre-Christian eras, as if the past two millennia were a mistake and their evaporation from human thinking the happy denouement of a long, silly plot. "We are in an ethical condition," wrote Bernard Williams without regret, "that lies not only beyond Christianity but beyond its Kantian and its Hegelian legacies."[2] Beyond Plato and Aristotle, too, he added.

In sociological terms, metaphysical man's disappearance severs us from the trajectory of human existence described in Plato's *Republic VII* and which was rightly regarded as the key to Western thought. Naturally, by disqualifying any record of metaphysical inquiry, we no longer feel the need to learn from it. As soon as we reject metaphysical inquiry, reducing it to nothing more than an impressive literary device, or relegating it to an epoch that allegedly we have moved beyond, we become intellectually men in chains.

In practice, it means an often slow process of "deculturalization," a somewhat clumsy word roughly corresponding to Plato's *apaideusia*. Certain totalitarian regimes, intent on enforcing conformity, consciously chose to replace metaphysics with political ideology, thus depriving citizens of their identity's transcendent roots. The result, whether achieved through brutal coercion, ideological pressure, spiritual *ennui*, or *nostalgie de la boue*, was always the same: the human mind was flattened and narrowed to the point where it was unable to reach beyond itself and gain a higher perspective.

As the hierarchical quest for higher understanding weakens, the concept of *paideia* loses its meaning. When human conduct is no longer motivated by some finality, when this finality no longer induces "ordinate affections," to quote C.S. Lewis, there is no need to build one's character according to nonfactual criteria. *Paideia* was always depicted as a process of attaining some objective ideal. Even if that ideal was political, moral, or social—that is, reality-based—it preserved its validity and attractiveness because of the metaphysical presumptions that loomed behind an individual's words and deeds.

Hierarchies collapse without this presumption. Words and deeds are considered self-expressions rather than attempts to reach out to something beyond oneself. From this new perspective, what matters is an ability to cooperate with others, adapt and conform, negotiate and compromise, and engage in power games. In such a society, politics and egalitarianism determine people's search for their real selves, not transcendence or metaphysics. The latter are condemned not only as delusions but as something worse; namely, a form of perfidiously camouflaged politics.

This is an entirely new world, one we have being living in for quite some time, and which we have grown so accustomed to that, like Plato's men in chains, we cannot imagine any other. What is qualitatively new about it is that the high/low distinction has ebbed from most areas of life. First of all, it has changed our view of life and death, the former now having no sanctity, the latter no mystery. Since the post-metaphysical men indignantly reject any suggestion that they might be deposed kings with objective obligations not of their own making, they do not feel particularly bound by the past or the future.

This change has spilled over into almost everything. There is no language in which we can express our higher aspirations, so no aspirations are high, all being equal. The same is true of our experiences and desires. The criteria that we use to praise or condemn something no longer distinguishes between high and low. Even churches and religions have adapted their forms of communication and liturgy to satisfy egalitarian sensibilities.

These consequences could have been expected because they mirror a non-metaphysical scenario in which everything is volatile and can be regulated only through the political process. However, an omnipresent feeling of ultimate senselessness debunks every hierarchical arrangement. Dostoyevsky was one of the first to envision such a scenario. There is a memorable episode in *The Possessed*. "Shatov declares that if there's to be a rising in Russia we must begin with atheism. Maybe it's true. One grizzled old stager of a captain sat mum, not saying a word. All at once he stands up in the middle of the room and says aloud, as though speaking to himself: *If there's no God, how can I be a captain then?* He took up his cap and went out, flinging up his hands."[3]

But there was a particularly eloquent and vociferous opposition to this scenario. The critics of *homo metaphysicus* predicted different consequences. True liberation came from being free of both God and metaphysics, they extolled, describing it in language similar to that of religious writers. God was replaced by Man, and Man's alleged independence and self-sufficiency were elevated to godlike freedom. "For in all things," wrote Bertrand Russell in his least antireligious text, *Free Man's Worship*, "it is well to exalt the dignity of Man, by freeing him as far as possible from the tyranny of non-human Power." He continued in the same quasi-religious rhetoric. "In this lies Man's true freedom: in determination to worship only the God created by our own love of the good, to respect only the heaven which inspires the insight of our best moments. In action, in desire, we must submit perpetually to the tyranny of outside forces; but in thought, in aspiration, we are free, free from our fellow-men, free from the petty planet on which our bodies impotently crawl, free even, while we live, from the tyranny of death."[4]

Nietzsche provided the most articulate exposition of this view. He was ambitious enough to replace both Platonic and Christian metaphysics with his own philosophy that retained a metaphysical structure. The chapters on Übermensch in *Thus Spake Zarathustra* could be read as a response to Plato's cave allegory. All the elements of Plato's narrative were there: a mob called "the last men" corresponded to the men in chains; there was a lonely protagonist, the Superman, whom the last men did not understand;

images of light and lightening appeared with his advent; and there was the high/low perspective, with the Übermensch representing the high. "Thus only groweth man aloft to the height where the lightning striketh and shattereth him:" wrote Nietzsche, "High enough for the lightning!"[5]

The crucial difference was that the Superman did not take his creative strength from metaphysics, which he abolished along with God, but from "the Earth". In *Gay Science* (*The Joyful Wisdom*), Nietzsche credited his Superman's superiority to his "great health," as compared with the infected biological constitution of metaphysicians and priests. The Superman ascended to new highs from the ruins of metaphysics and Christianity, so marking the dawn of a new era. "Whoever is born after us—for the sake of this deed [the killing of God] he will belong to a higher history than all history hitherto," wrote Nietzsche.[6]

Whether Nietzsche really believed in the coming of the Superman was a moot point. But at the time, the concept of the Superman captured the imaginations of important writers such as George Bernard Shaw and Thomas Mann, both of whom were inclined to believe in the dawn of a new epoch. The idea of greatness cloaked in a new historical costume seemed particularly seductive in an era rife with exhaustion and mediocrity.

Nietzsche's Superman not only failed to materialize but his concept fell out of favor, not least because of its eventual association with Hitler's ideology of German supremacy. Needless to say, Nietzsche might have committed many philosophical sins, but this was not one of them. However, it could be argued he was partly to blame for this association due to his enticing but sloppy writing and contempt for theoretical consistency.

Paradoxically, instead of being reinvigorated by Superman's quasi-divine self-expression, Western societies moved in the opposite direction. Interestingly, Nietzsche had accurately predicted such a development when he wrote about "the new species of man," "that contemptible thing," "ineradicable like the ground-flea," and "the last man who maketh everything small." These last men did indeed materialize, or rather gathered forces and acquired unprecedented power. And they had a rather warm reception, at least if we judge from how Francis Fukuyama wrote about them in his *End of History and the Last Man*, and how he interpreted their role in the modern world.

The Russellian/Nietzschean *paideia* could not work. Their lofty language was nothing more than a verbal trick, and the Superman a rhetorical artifact with no possibility of life. Whoever drove out the metaphysical dimension from human nature took a step towards the minimalist concept of the self. The last men fell precisely into this category. They indeed did a lot of good things, like those people from the feast parable who received the invitation but "made light of it, and went their ways, one to his own farm, another to his merchandise," (Mat. 22:14). But, as it has been argued above, they were unable to cope with the formidable forces that subdue human wills and minds.

Russell, Nietzsche, and their ilk, who liberated man from "the tyranny of non-human power" in the hope of opening up breathtaking vistas for him, should not have been surprised that ultimately it was the man "who maketh everything small" that turned out victorious. These philosophers did not liberate man, but stripped an essential part of his identity away from him. C.S. Lewis put it just right. "In a sort of ghastly simplicity, we remove the organ and demand the function. We make men without chests and expect of them virtue and enterprise. We laugh at honor and are shocked to find traitors in our midst. We castrate and bid the geldings be fruitful."[7]

CONCLUSION

Though the three types of freedom are different from one another, they can overlap both conceptually and in reality. This is what makes both the concept and the experience of freedom confusing. Many people desire liberty, but after they gain it they often feel dissatisfied; not that it is not enough, but that it is not quite what they imagined. Some may have free space but unfortunately lack the power to strive for their goals. Others may have such power, but feel alienated because they are serving somebody else's goals and are not even sure what it means to be themselves. No matter how many rights the courts and legislatures grant, the dominant feeling in a free society is uneasiness.

We are told that our society is free. This was not a controversial statement when it referred to the Western world while totalitarian regimes occupied half of Europe and most of Asia. Even though these regimes now are gone (at least in Europe) this statement does not seem self-evident; nor does it mean that its opposite—ours is an unfree society—is unqualifiedly true. For many years, every Western society has declared freedom paramount. It has been hailed, cherished, glorified, and included in constitutions and political agendas—all of this (or nearly all of this) quite sincerely. It would be unthinkable for anyone, particularly politicians and lawmakers, to disqualify freedom and minimize its role. True, its meaning has been tampered with, distorted, reduced, and stretched, but it continues to be an article of faith for all and sundry. From schoolchildren to professors, engineers to artists, manual workers to farmers, everyone wants to be free in some sense or another.

Yet this enthusiastic pro-liberty rhetoric and activity has not resulted in an easing of freedom-related tensions and their accompanying sense of ambiguity. Our society has created a system in which we, individually and collectively, insist on being free. However, to secure that freedom we have had to accept laws, ideas, mechanisms, institutions, and technical devices that we fear are beyond our control. We are increasingly afraid of being manipulated, losing our autonomy, being indoctrinated and over-regulated, or threatened by known and unknown forces. All of this in a civilization that proclaims itself to be the freest ever known. Yet our fears are not irrational.

Earlier in this book, I indicated one problem that has become particularly acute: the growing influence of liberalism and how it controls negative freedom's distribution. I pointed out how liberalism, as a specific political doctrine, has coalesced into liberalism as a super-theory that has enforced itself on modern society as the best regulator of human diversity. All attempts to deprive liberalism of its imperial bent, such as John Rawls's "political liberalism," have failed. It does not matter whether liberalism follows Rawls's social democratic model, if it is more market-oriented, or even anarcho-libertarian. In each version, the problem remains the same. The following scenario might be perhaps the best way to elucidate it.

Imposing the liberal system of freedom requires that the disadvantaged receive more free space while the privileged have a certain amount of it taken away from them. Some form of social engineering is necessary to achieve this, if only to upgrade particular groups, individuals, opinions, or practices while restraining others; for instance, upgrading women and blacks while restraining patriarchy. This calls for a certain degree of coercion, or at least energetic persuasion. Typically, this is directed against the bulwarks of conservatism and other forms of petrified privileges such as entrenched ways of life, allegedly anachronistic beliefs, traditional divisions, and supposedly sacrosanct norms, etc.

To eliminate their influence, governments have to launch intensive educational programs, preferably starting at the earliest level such as in kindergartens. They place particular emphasis on the use of language as well as which appropriate books, films, games, and Internet sites can inculcate the mechanisms of a new, freer society. There must be new standards of writing that are as open and as inclusive as possible so that no one feels estranged. But since the laws that secure freedom have to be changed too, there is always the possibility that they might be used against those who stubbornly refuse to abide.

Admittedly, such a transformation may be painful sometimes. Nevertheless, its advocates claim it is necessary. After all, the history of mankind is a history of discrimination: whites against blacks, men against women, Europeans against non-Europeans, heterosexuals against homosexuals, etc. Therefore, many pitfalls lurk in the process of creating a free society: sexism, racism, anti-Semitism, Islamophobia, binary thinking, misogyny, ageism, homophobia, and speciesism. The list is incomplete because new forms of discrimination are being continually discovered, and all of them have to be monitored and curbed. No wonder that freedom's friends should employ every instrument at their disposal, from law to social ostracism. According to the new system's apologists, opponents of the transformation process do not deserve compassion.

The above description looks like a caricature, but it is not. The liberal order requires social engineering to be implemented and this, in turn, means not only restructuring society but marginalizing those who oppose the process. As an example, let us take the new concept of marriage, which is said to no longer be restrictive but now far more "inclusive" because it has ceased to be defined as a union between a man and a woman. Naturally, this revolutionary change has been met with opposition from various groups, and its opponents have a variety of good arguments–biological, moral, historical, etc. Western civilization's attachment to marriage as a union of one man and one woman is profoundly rooted in its social and moral fabric. Polygamy and group marriage have always been rejected and condemned, and monogamy makes sense only if it is between a man and a woman. The union of two men or two women is as good or as bad as the group marriage of several men and several women. Thus, if we accept group marriage among people of the same sex, why forbid it for people of different sexes, especially since sex has changed into "gender" which, we have been informed, has myriad variations and is as multicolored as a rainbow?

To overcome opposition to the "inclusive" concept of marriage, governments, courts, and interest groups have used very strong, even brutal means. Marriages and families based on the union of two sexes—until recently regarded as the most solid pillar of social order—are now called "traditional," with the implication being that they are destined for historical oblivion. Marriage has changed, as one liberal scholar put it, from "procreational" to "relational." In addition, we have been informed that it has changed for a reason: too often marriage has been an oppressive institution, full of domestic violence, husbands raping wives and daughters, and women being trampled by patriarchal structures. The only solution has been to loosen the legal and customary ties that have kept "traditional marriage" and the family together. Thus, state institutions have been equipped with special rights to intervene in cases where they have deemed them necessary.

Simultaneously, the legal regulations surrounding this new "inclusive" marriage have become increasingly intrusive. Once the law has been passed, either through legislation or court rulings, it has been ruthlessly enforced—the argument being that under no circumstances can it be broken. Since the state does not tolerate tax evasion or plagiarism, why should it tolerate contempt for the same-sex marriage law?

Indeed, state institutions have proved they mean it. Consciences have been violated, institutions that have disagreed have been punished, dissenters have been widely ostracized, and Orwellian spectacles have been staged to intimidate potential objectors. Fewer people have been able to hide behind conscience clauses; adoption centers that have resisted have been dismantled; priests and pastors loyal to their calling have been threatened with lawsuits and sometimes taken to court. A gigantic propaganda machine (generously supported by major corporations) has

begun to mercilessly alter people's minds, starting with children in kin-
dergarten. Mainstream culture has duly complied with the overall trend.
All institutions that have questioned this revolutionary change, including
the Catholic Church and other moral institutions, have been vilified.
Twitter mobs hunt for heretics. Those few individuals who have dared
to say "no" have usually lost their jobs and became objects of verbal, even
physical abuse.

These and similar processes have had a debilitating effect on people's
minds not only because the propaganda has been effective, but primarily
because they have destroyed the language of communication and reversed
the meaning of basic concepts. From the very beginning, liberalism has
made itself the sole champion of liberty, pluralism, tolerance, and diversity, and the ardent enemy of discrimination, intolerance, and exclusion.
This etymological trick–the word "liberalism" stems from "*libertas*," the
Latin word for freedom–has worked perfectly. Encyclopedias, handbooks,
political and historical treaties, all take it for granted that liberalism and
freedom go hand in hand. Even our everyday language reflects this: when
we say "a liberal approach" or "the law was liberalized," we always associate
it with greater freedom.

No wonder that once liberalism became the ruling doctrine, it was
generally assumed that with its increasing influence we would have far
more liberty, pluralism, tolerance, and diversity, and far less discrimination,
intolerance, and exclusion. Any action dressed up in liberal jargon has been
automatically interpreted as favoring freedom and being antidiscriminatory.
No matter how brutal those actions have been, no matter how much they
have violated consciences, harnessed free inquiry or debate, or humiliated
people, they have all been presented and accepted as serving freedom's
cause. The minority who have had some doubts have blamed the negative
side effects on progressivism, postmodernism, and many other -isms, while
liberalism has remained unblemished. How can liberalism hinder liberty?
they have asked in disbelief. Regardless of quarrels over definition, those
who have protested these scandalous measures have been condemned

as bigots, reactionaries, and fascists who want to turn back the clock of history and reintroduce the Spanish Inquisition. This last sentence is not an exaggeration. It illustrates the standard manner in which liberals talk about their opponents.

We have become so used to this argument and rhetoric that we have failed to notice how it has affected our language and warped the meaning of the words we use. Formerly, such concepts as pluralism, diversity, tolerance, and openness were intended to soften human interaction and to temper the strictness of the political and moral order. They also sheltered those who felt excessively dominated by others. Today, these words have acquired a sinister meaning. The erstwhile soft concepts have turned into ideological sticks with which to bludgeon opponents. They no longer provide shelter; they intimidate because they now mean the exact opposite. Pluralism means monopoly; diversity–conformity; tolerance–censorship; openness–ideological rigidity. In just about every private or public institution, school, or corporation, there are offices responsible for diversity, tolerance, and pluralism. All of them are gruesome ideological agencies, spreading fear and imposing conformity, not unlike their inglorious Communist predecessors.

This is not only a matter of oppression. This is a form of corruption that touches the deepest layers of our intellectual faculties and prevents us from utilizing them. Since pluralism no longer means a variety of different opinions, but the domination of liberalism (which its adherents believe to be pluralist by definition), the ultimate implementation of pluralism will be the absolute triumph of liberalism, and the absolute triumph of liberalism will be the ultimate implementation of pluralism. It will be a society in which everyone will be a liberal and, *ipso facto* a pluralist. Absolute pluralism will be the absolute monopoly of one ideology. Or to put it differently, the world will be safe for pluralism only if there is unanimity of opinions.

Unfortunately, this seemingly absurd conclusion is not a harmless logical quip but is becoming a fact. Examples are not hard to find. There are European countries where all the media share a single ideology. Not surprisingly, the absence of a platform for non-liberal opinions has never troubled the European Union, the Council of Europe, any European or national tribunals, or influential NGOs. On the contrary, this has come to be generally regarded as a natural and positive state of affairs and a model to be emulated by those countries that lag behind. What is not considered normal and what rouses concern is that in some places this monopoly has yet to be cemented or, even worse, that in certain places it can be jeopardized. Today's liberalism adopts a version of the Brezhnev doctrine: any threat to liberal dominance anywhere is a threat to liberalism everywhere, justifying immediate and forceful intervention by any means necessary. Therefore, fire is directed at countries such as Poland where unanimity across the media has disappeared and there is a real pluralism of opinions spanning left to right. From the ruling liberal orthodoxy's point of view, this is apparently the wrong kind of pluralism and should be abolished, while the lost territory should be reconquered.

One of the powerful ways in which this monopoly sustains itself is its remarkable ability to identify new enemies that are seen as threatening freedom from all sides. In fact, this monopoly feeds itself on what Orwell called "thoughtcrimes." Today's thoughtcrimes, as I mentioned above, are many and growing in number: sexism, racism, Islamophobia, binary thinking, misogyny, and homophobia are just a few. What is shocking is that this number is far greater than the Communist system's number of thoughtcrimes which, one would have thought, was unbeatable given its determination to unearth enemies and destroy them. But, apparently, liberalism has surpassed it. The dense system of taboos, thou-shalt-nots, and crooked redlines has created a particularly unpleasant environment for the human mind, and prevents it from roaming freely out of sheer curiosity in pursuit of the truth. The only prudent strategy one can take in this environment is to avoid ideological booby traps. All of them are deadly.

The big question is not only why is this happening, but why is there so little resistance to the massive mendacity surrounding us? Possible answers may be found in the second and third parts of this book. The second section concludes that we have neglected Aristotle's concept of the free man and forgotten about its importance. The third part's conclusion is that we have abandoned the strong concept of the self by mistakenly assuming freedom is more congruent with a minimalist concept of the human self. Those two errors have made us vulnerable to the pernicious consequences of the liberal distribution of negative freedom and insensitive to the destruction of language. The two errors have melted into one. We have assumed that fortifying individuals with rights is enough, thus eliminating the problem of the free man and the self. It is not.

Despite occasional associations with remnants of old, half-forgotten views, the concept of the rights-bearing individual no longer denotes anything concrete, probably out of a belief that it can denote anything. Being unaware of how difficult it is to acquire the status of a free man, most people accept liberalism because it offers an easy and comfortable solution. Its alluring power lies in a combination of two factors. On the one hand, it is meant to address people as individuals, telling them that everyone has both the right and the freedom to become whomever and whatever they want. On the other hand, liberalism is a political system that secures those rights, bolstered by an ideology that regulates people's conduct, tells them right from wrong, what to love and who to hate. The combination of these two elements generates a seemingly self-evident conclusion that one should fully identify with the system in order to be free, then the system will reciprocate by enlarging freedom for everyone. Blending into this system is a natural outcome, given the relatively high degree of loneliness that characterizes the world of negative freedom.

It's a highly disconcerting conclusion. The whole point of the free man was not that he was defined by the sheer absence of obstacles—and being defined by rights falls into this category—but that his freedom was positive. He had to meet clear moral criteria that would enable him to direct his life in an objectively valuable way, and for this he had to have a larger view of himself and the world around him. Therefore, he derived inspiration from outside the political system in which he lived, not necessarily in direct opposition to it, but mostly independently of it.

In Aristotle, the free man came from ethics and anthropology, and only in small part from the structure of the city-state.

The philosopher and the artist came from outside the system, too, being the products of certain philosophical concepts that ran counter to the prevailing sociopolitical reality and its ideology. Over the course of time, however, the paradigm adapted to this reality, even though it still fed on old myths of superiority and independence that no longer had any relevance to what philosophers and artists were doing. Even the entrepreneur, being the product of the capitalist system, somehow believed himself to be subject to a different order until he, too, capitulated and chose the road of conformity. The concept of the aristocrat reappeared occasionally, and although wise people strongly supported it, it never found its way into the hearts and minds of society at large, while liberal democratic folklore disparaged and ridiculed it.

A man fortified by his rights is entirely immersed in, and dependent upon, the political system. He must be deeply indebted to it because the system gives him his rights, and without these he is nothing. He expresses whatever misgivings he might have about the system in the language of rights and other liberal democratic paraphernalia. Though grateful for his rights, he often becomes angry; he is disappointed by his expected benefits and wants the system to do better.

But if a good human life requires certain principles—such as honor, a sense of duty and of shame, or certain notions about the human soul— that his own system does not value highly, he would rather acquiesce to prevailing stereotypes than steer towards the principles that would make him a free man. If his society genuflects before false idols such as a belief in modernization's inexorability and the sanctity of rights, he will eagerly join the worshippers and refrain from critiquing the political cults.

But without clear alternative views of what it means to be a free man, his chances of becoming one are slim. Internally, he is too weak, too dependent on external factors, too confused about his identity, and too attracted to this view of himself. He will not seek alternatives until he abandons the liberal tradition's founding assumption that freedom is only compatible with a thin concept of the self. This is probably one of the most rigid dogmas to have contaminated our thinking since liberalism began its offensive.

The argument to support it sounds commonsensical, at first, but it is misleading. People with stronger selves, such as nationalists or believers in a higher order, are said to be intransigent in their staunch convictions and therefore are forever trying to impose their beliefs on others. The liberal man (protected by his rights) fears these people, firstly because he has been taught to fear them as the villains and perpetrators of every evil from slavery to the concentration camps, and secondly because he believes himself to be the guardian of openness and compromise.

There might be some truth in the argument about intransigence, but that is beside the point. The theory which justifies strong assertions may be intransigent, to be sure, but the theory which justifies weak claims may be equally, or even more so. Though they have a thin view of the human self, liberals are also intransigent in their views and, in their tireless mission to track down innumerable authoritarianisms, are very unwilling to reach a compromise with anyone. Locke was more dogmatic than Burke, though his view of man was minimalist whereas Burke's was not. Jean-Paul Sartre (who, it will be recalled, denied the human self's existence), was not a man of compromise and took a rather hard line defending the Communist system. All in all, the statement seems like another version of the trick described above, namely, that a theory hijacks soft concepts and uses them as an excuse to strengthen its hardline ideology. If this theory claims the values of tolerance and moderation for itself, then its advocates believe they can enforce it quite ruthlessly on others because, in so doing, they are enforcing tolerance and moderation. In certain respects, this replicates Rousseau's idea that an effective government should force an individual to be free by subjecting him to the general will.

The thin view of the self may function as an aggressive tool against denser, more complex views; it may even generate obsessive hatred which one hears today in the language of identity politics. It may mobilize supporters and give them some kind of ideological orientation in the world–a false one, but one that unites them effectively for a political purpose. It can destroy true historical and social bonds among people, vulgarize their cultural environment, and water down their moral consciences. What it cannot do however is give people a fairly stable sense of freedom. Despite the countless rights and ideological exhortations, people half suspect and half fear that they are performing in a play that they neither wrote, nor directed, and that their role is not a genuine imprint of their true selves.

NOTES

INTRODUCTION

1 Isaiah Berlin, *Four Essays on Liberty* (Oxford: Oxford University Press, 1979), 133.

2 Berlin, *Four Essays*, 154.

PART ONE — NEGATIVE FREEDOM

CHAPTER THREE: MAXIMUM FREEDOM

1 Jean-Jacques Rousseau, *The Social Contract and Discourses by Jean-Jacques Rousseau* trans. by G.D.H. Cole (London and Toronto: J.M. Dent & Sons, 1923), https://oll.libertyfund.org/titles/rousseau -the-social-contract-and-discourses.

2 Thomas Hobbes, *Leviathan* (New York: Collier, 1977), 98.

3 Hobbes, *Leviathan*, 100.

4 To John Paul II's statement that "obedience to the truth about God and man is the first condition of freedom", Milton Friedman's reply was "Whose 'truth'? Decided by whom? Echoes of the Spanish Inquisition?" https://miltonfriedman.hoover.org /friedman_images/Collections/2016c21/NR_06_24_1991.pdf

5 Ronald Dworkin et al., "Assisted Suicide: Philosophers' Brief," *The New York Review of Books*, March 27, 1997.

6 https://www.macleans.ca/politics/ottawa/chrystia-freeland-on -canadas-foreign-policy-full-speech/

7 https://agendaeurope.files.wordpress.com/2014/11/funding_of _abortion_through_eu_development_aid_full_version.pdf

8   Hobbes, *Leviathan*, 103.

9   United States Congress, *The Declaration of Independence* (1776) https://www.archives.gov/founding-docs/declaration-transcript

10 U.S. Congress, *The Declaration of Independence*

11 Ignacy Potocki, King Stanislaw August, Fr. Hugo Kottataj, *The Constitution of the 3rd of May* (1791), http://polishfreedom.pl /en/document/constitution-of-the-3rd-of-may-1791-the -government-statute

12 The United Nations General Assembly, *The Universal Declaration of Human Rights* (1948), https://www.un.org/en/universal -declaration-human-rights/index.html

13 U.S. Congress, *The Declaration of Independence*

CHAPTER FOUR: FREEDOM FROM TYRANNY

1   *The Un-Divine Comedy, and Other Poems* by the Anonymous Poet of Poland, Count Sigismund Krasinski, trans. by Martha Walker Cook (Philadelphia: Lippincott 1875) https://archive.org/details /undivinecomedyotookras/page/n7/mode/2up

2   Tadeusz Kroński, *Zaraz po wojnie* (Krakow: Znak, 1999), 318. Kroński, a Polish Marxist-Stalinist philosopher used this phrase in a letter written in 1948 to the Polish poet and essayist, Czesław Miłosz, a 1980 Nobel Prize winner in literature.

3   Edmund Burke, *Reflections on the Revolution in France* (Penguin Books 1979), 194-195.

4   Michael Oakeshott, *On Human Conduct* (Oxford: Clarendon Press 1991), 128.

5   Michael Oakeshott, "The Voice of Poetry in the Conversation of Mankind," in: *Rationalism in Politics and Other Essays* (London and New York: Methuen 1981) 197-247.

6   House of Commons of Canada, *Bill C-16, An Act to amend the Canadian Human Rights Act and the Criminal Code* (First Session, Forty-second Parliament, 2015-2016), https://www.parl.ca /DocumentViewer/en/42-1/bill/C-16/first-reading.

7 Jeanne Smits, "France passes law imposing up to two years prison for running pro-life websites," Life Site News, Feb 17, 2017, https://www.lifesitenews.com/news/france-approves-restrictive-law -targeting-pro-life-websites.

8 Immanuel Kant, *What Is Enlightenment,* https://resources.saylor. org/wwwresources/archived/site/wp-content/uploads/2011/02 /What-is-Enlightenment.pdf

PART TWO — POSITIVE FREEDOM

CHAPTER SIX: THE PHILOSOPHER

1 Lucius Annaeus Seneca, *Moral Epistles, Volume II,* trans. by Richard M. Gummere (The Loeb Classical Library, Cambridge: Harvard University Press, 1917-25), epistle 88 "On Liberal Views and Vocational Studies," http://www.stoics.com/seneca_epistles _book_2.html#'LXXXVIII1.

2 John Henry Newman, *The Idea of a University* (Notre Dame: Notre Dame University Press, 1982), 126.

CHAPTER SEVEN: THE ENTREPRENEUR

1 Michael Novak, "Two Moral Ideas for Business," *Three in One: Essays on Democratic Capitalism 1976-2000* (Lanham: Rowman and Littlefield, 2001), 227.

2 Max Weber, *The Protestant Ethic and the Spirit of Capitalism* (New York: Charles Scribner's Sons, 1958), 112.

3 Weber, *Protestant,* 115.

4 Weber, *Protestant,* 181-182.

5 Max Horkheimer, *Eclipse of Reason* (New York: Oxford University Press, 1947), 128.

CHAPTER EIGHT: THE ARTIST

1 Henri Bergson, *Creative Evolution,* trans. by Arthur Mitchel (Gutenberg Project e-book, 2008), https://www.gutenberg.org /files/26163/26163-h/26163-h.htm.

2 F.W.J. Schelling, *Philosophical Investigations into the Essence of Human Freedom*, trans. by Jeff Love and Johannes Schmidt (Albany: State University of New York Press, 2006), 51.

3 Thomas Carlyle, *Characteristics*, Ed. Charles W. Eliot, The Harvard Classics, Vol. 25 (New York: Collier, 1909), 333-371, https://cruel. org/econthought/texts/carlyle/carlchar.html.

4 Lord Byron, *Manfred* (Act II, Scene II), https://resources.saylor .org/wwwresources/archived/site/wp-content/uploads/2014/06 /ENGL404-Lord-Byron-Manfred.pdf

5 Paul Kegan, *Richard Wagner's Prose Works*, Ed. William Ashton Ellis (London: Trench, Trubner & Co., 1895), https://archive.org /stream/richardwagnerspro11341mbp/richardwagnerspro11341mbp _djvu.txt

CHAPTER NINE: THE ARISTOCRAT

1 Plato, *Gorgias*, trans. by Terence Irwin (Oxford, Clarendon Press, 1979), 505a-b.

2 Plato, *The Republic of Plato*, trans. by Allan Bloom (New York: Basic Books, 1991), 573a4-c9, 565d9-566a4, 571c3-d4, 493a9-b5.

PART THREE — INNER FREEDOM

CHAPTER ELEVEN: THE NONEXISTENT SELF

1 David Hume, *A Treatise of Human Nature*, ed. L.A. Selby-Bigge (Oxford: Clarendon Press, 1896), sec. 6, https://oll.libertyfund.org /titles/hume-a-treatise-of-human-nature.

2 David Hume, *Enquiry Concerning Human Understanding*, sec. 5, https://www.earlymoderntexts.com/assets/pdfs/hume1748.pdf.

3 Blaise Pascal, *Pensées*, trans. W.F. Trotter (Grand Rapids: Christian Classics Ethereal Library, 2002), 323 https://d2y1pz2y630308. cloudfront.net/15471/documents/2016/10/Blaise%20Pascal-%20 Pensees.pdf.

4 Blaise Pascal, *Pensées* (Paris: Chez Guillaume Desprez, 1671), sec

. 29, "Pensées Morales," http://kaempfer.free.fr/oeuvres/pdf
/pascal-pensees.pdf.

5 Pascal, *Pensées*, https://d2y1pz2y630308.cloudfront.net/15471
   /documents/2016/10/Blaise%20Pascal-%20Pensees.pdf.

6 Pascal, *Pensées*, https://d2y1pz2y630308.cloudfront.net/15471
   /documents/2016/10/Blaise%20Pascal-%20Pensees.pdf.

7 Jean-Paul Sartre, *La Nausée*, (Paris: Éditions Gallimard, 1938), 125.

8 Jean-Paul Sartre, "Existentialism is a Humanism." Lecture given
   by the author in 1946. trans. by Philip Mairet, http://www
   .mrsmoser.com/uploads/8/5/0/1/8501319/english_11_ib_-_no_
   exit_-_existentialism_is_a_humanism_-_sartre.pdf.

9 Jean-Paul Sartre, *Being and Nothingness* (New York: Washington
   Square Press, 1966), 694.

10 Albert Camus, *The Rebel* (New York: Vintage Books, 1956), 303,
   https://laurenralpert.files.wordpress.com/2014/08/camus-the
   -rebel.pdf.

11 Camus, *The Rebel*, 171.

CHAPTER TWELVE: THE MINIMAL SELF

1 Hobbes, *Leviathan*, 80.

2 Immanuel Kant, *Critique of Practical Reason* (Indianapolis
   /Cambridge: Hackett, 2002), 44.

3 John Stuart Mill, *Utilitarianism* (Kitchener, Ontario: Batoche
   Books, 2001), 13.

4 Frederick Engels, Karl Marx, *Communist Manifesto* (published
   online by Socialist Labor Party of America, 2006), http://www.slp
   .org/pdf/marx/comm_man.pdf.

5 G.W.F. Hegel, *Phenomenology of Spirit* (Oxford: Oxford University
   Press, 1977), 318.

6 Plato, Republic, 561c6-d7.

7 John Locke, *A Letter Concerning Toleration* (The Federalist Papers
   Project), https://www.thefederalistpapers.org/wp-content

/uploads/2012/12/John-Locke-A-Letter-Concerning-Toleration
.pdf.

8   Hobbes, *Leviathan*, 239.

CHAPTER THIRTEEN: A STRONG CONCEPT OF SELF

1   Bernard Williams, *Shame and Necessity* (Berkeley: University of
California Press, 1994), 166.

2   Fyodor Dostoevsky, *The Possessed*, trans. by Constance Garnett
(The Project Gutenberg, 2005), https://www.gutenberg.org/files
/8117/8117-h/8117-h.htm.

3   Bertrand Russell, "A Free Man's Worship." An essay written
in 1903 from *Contemplation and Action, The Collected Papers of
Bertrand Russell*, Vol. 12. (London; now published by Routledge,
1985), https://www.skeptic.ca/Bertrand_Russell_Collection.pdf.

4   Friedrich Nietzsche, *Thus Spake Zarathustra*, trans. Thomas
Common (The Project Gutenberg, 1998), https://www.gutenberg
.org/files/1998/1998-h/1998-h.htm.

5   Friedrich Nietzsche, *The Gay Science* (New York: Vintage Books,
1974), 181.

6   C.S. Lewis, *The Abolition of Man* (Oxford: Oxford University
Press, 1943), https://archive.org/stream/TheAbolitionOfMan
_229/C.s.Lewis-TheAbolitionOfMan#page/n7/mode/2up.

INDEX